Assisted Dying

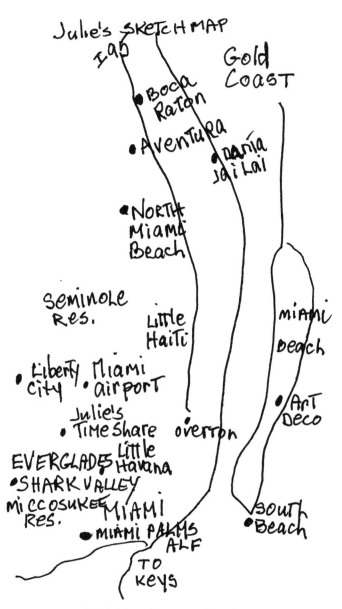

Julie's Map of Florida's Gold Coast

Assisted Dying

An Ethnographic Murder Mystery on Florida's Gold Coast

SERENA NANDA AND JOAN GREGG

ALTAMIRA
PRESS
A Division of
ROWMAN & LITTLEFIELD PUBLISHERS, INC.
Lanham • New York • Toronto • Plymouth, UK

Published by AltaMira Press
A division of Rowman & Littlefield Publishers, Inc.
A wholly owned subsidary of The Rowman & Littlefield Publishing Group, Inc.
4501 Forbes Boulevard, Suite 200, Lanham, Maryland 20706
http://www.altamirapress.com

Estover Road, Plymouth PL6 7PY, United Kingdom

British Library Cataloguing in Publication Information Available

Library of Congress Cataloging-in-Publication Data

Nanda, Serena.
  Assisted dying : an ethnographic murder mystery on Florida's gold coast / Serena
Nanda and Joan Gregg.
    p. cm.
  Includes bibliographical references.
  ISBN 978-0-7591-1994-9 (cloth : alk. paper) — ISBN 978-0-7591-1995-6 (pbk. : alk.
paper) — ISBN 978-0-7591-1996-3 (electronic)
  1. Aging—Fiction. 2. Anthropology—Fiction. 3. Florida—Fiction. I. Gregg, Joan
Young. II. Title.

  PS3613.A579A93 2011
  813'.6—dc22   2010049512

∞™ The paper used in this publication meets the minimum requirements of
American National Standard for Information Sciences—Permanence of Paper for
Printed Library Materials, ANSI/NISO Z39.48-1992.

Printed in the United States of America

To Alan McClare

Contents

Our novel is an ethnographically informed fiction. The specific situations and characters, with the exception of media reports of public events or anthropologists referred to in the text, are all products of the authors' imaginations. Any resemblance to actual persons or events is wholly coincidental.

🌴 Authors' Note

The South Florida Gold Coast encapsulates the core patterns of American culture and society over the past century. Through plot, dialogue, and character development, our novel examines America's economic ideologies, family values, cultural diversity, and its various expressions of social stratification. In highlighting some of the ideals and realities of various Gold Coast communities regarding aging, retirement, health care practices, death and dying, and perhaps above all, the multifaceted pursuit of the American Dream, our story of the Gold Coast is an American story.

South Florida Gold Coast residents are unexpectedly and mysteriously dying—in nursing homes, hospitals, and in their own beds—from a variety of unknown causes. Relatives and medical personnel become persons of interest in these suspicious deaths, which may well be homicides. Our protagonist, Julie Norman, a cultural anthropology professor at a major New York City university, is drawn into the case through the death of her elderly aunt. Her academic background and previous ethnographic research (*The Gift of a Bride: A Tale of Anthropology, Matrimony, and Murder*) in American and immigrant communities provide her with cultural perspectives that inform the foundation of our narrative.

Implicit throughout *Assisted Dying* is the utopian vision of the (ad)venture capitalist Henry Flagler, who first recognized the potential of South

Florida's Gold Coast as America's last frontier. By developing its agriculture and infrastructure, including a coastal railroad that would eventually extend all the way to Key West, Flagler transformed South Florida into a place where millions of Americans would try to fulfill the ideal of their well-earned "golden years." Especially after World War II, the region's comfortable climate, inexpensive real estate, low taxes, and burgeoning medical facilities enticed the ill and the elderly as temporary or permanent residents. Immigrants, too, fleeing poor economic and political conditions in their homelands, found opportunities there for unskilled work and upward mobility. However, the Gold Coast also attracted its share of the greedy and the predatory, whose various schemes and scams victimized each of these groups and pitted them against each other for their own purposes. The unregulated profit motive of some health care and social service providers to the elderly; the uncertain spaces occupied by the various ethnic groups staffing these services; and a powerful political and economic strata that privileged medical and business developers in a complex culture of indigenous communities, retirees, and patients all intersect in the dramatic action of the novel.

Utilizing anthropological and ethnographic methodology and her beguiling connections to law enforcement in the person of Detective Mike Cardella, our protagonist, Julie, draws the reader of *Assisted Dying* into a deeper understanding of the subculture of Florida's Gold Coast, where so many strands of American culture are played out: individualism, pragmatism, optimism, capitalism, social mobility, voluntarism, environmentalism, economic development, patriotism, and a sense of justice as well. But American culture also includes excessive consumerism, environmental exploitation, a propensity for violence, and a capacity for denial. These less laudatory values are also given an authentic and compelling human face throughout the novel's exploration of contemporary social, political, and economic issues.

In American college classrooms, particularly over the past twenty years, alternative and creative forms of ethnographic presentation—novels, poetry, memoirs, and oral histories—have become increasingly popular as a means of engaging our students in the disciplines of cultural and medical anthropology, sociology, psychology, ethnic studies, American studies, gender, gerontology, and other social sciences. To further this aim, we have extended the social and cultural content of each chapter in the bibliographic essay with citations for further reading as well as discussion questions. A glossary of social science concepts and foreign words and a map of Florida's Gold Coast are also included.

Many states are noted for just one attribute. . . . Like one state is known for its potatoes; one state is known for its oil . . . and another state like Florida is known for the old people.

—*Arnold Schwarzenegger, governor of California*

[The American] people want to see . . . retirement communities not as warehouses for the lonely, but as a Club Med with ramps.

—*Alessandra Stanley, in a review of* Sunset Daze

I will prescribe regimens for the good of my patients . . . and never do harm to anyone.

—*Hippocratic oath*

Chapter One

January 1, 2009, 4:00 a.m.
At this hour of the night, the hospital corridors were only dimly lit, and the nurses' station was quiet. Only a lone attendant sat at her computer, intently transferring data from patients' folders onto the screen in front of her. A tall figure in a white coat stood at the darkened entrance to the now empty visitors' lounge and peered out, swiveling his head rapidly down the hallways at either side. The green uniformed orderly who worked the robot carts was nowhere in sight. The white-coated figure ventured out into the hallway and slipped around the nurses' station under the attendant's radar into the corridor that housed the patients' rooms. Removing a scrap of paper from his pocket, he used a small penlight to carefully scan the slotted doorplates above each patient's room for the names written largely in black marker. When he saw the name he wanted, almost at the end of the hallway, he quickly looked behind him for the night-shift orderly who worked this maze of corridors, but he was still not to be seen.

Drawing on latex gloves, the white-coated figure gently opened the door to the room, then silently entered, closing it with an almost undetectable click. As he slipped inside, he turned off his penlight, regarding the patient in a deep coma, who was hooked up to the life support machine. *Life support*, the man sneered to himself, *who can call this life! This guy is dead*

1

meat, in more ways than one, he chuckled as he quietly removed a pillow from a chair near the bed and held it over the patient's nose and mouth. After a few minutes, when he assured himself the man was dead—*really dead, not that so-called brain dead folks invented in yet another denial of death*—the white-coated man swiftly exited the room into the corridor.

Good, hallway and exit stairs empty. The staircase down was hard on his bad leg, but at this hour it was deserted and he could take it a little bit easy. Following his practiced evasion route, he remained invisible to the security guard and made certain he was not observed walking outside to the parking lot. Hunkering down in his car, he stripped off his white coat and sped out of sight. Well away from the hospital, he stopped by the curb of a "pump your own" gas station, flipped up his cell, speed-dialed a number, and left a terse message: "fresh meat delivery tomorrow as expected." At this wee hour of New Year's Eve, with hardly any cars on the road, the man relaxed at the wheel, congratulating himself on his night's takings. *This should be enough to keep the goons at bay for a while,* he hoped, giving little thought to the life he had just snuffed out. *Americans fear dying,* he reflected; *they want to live forever, even in a coma that could last for years, or addled by Alzheimer's. They need to have a body to bury, even for their pets. It's on all the TV crime shows. Hell, their body parts make them worth a lot more dead than alive.* With his connection at the funeral home, the real dirty work of buying and selling left him with clean hands: a fresh cadaver and up, up, and away—American capitalism at its best. And he'd really lucked out with that illegal he met in the emergency room. The guy was so desperate for money he agreed—okay, not happily—to truck the merchandise to the airport when they needed him, no questions asked. He would make sure that the funeral director wouldn't forget that little favor the next time he made a delivery.

His mental accounting was momentarily interrupted by a shard of annoyance at that damned anthropologist and her noisy campaign about what she called "trafficking in body parts." *What the hell does an anthropologist know about it? Why can't they stick to studying those exotic Pacific Islands? Isn't that what they get paid for?* This "interfering witch" had already gotten the FBI involved, and they'd arrested some big guns. *Crazy,* he thought. *This is a win-win business. Useless folks make a contribution to science; this stuff ad-vances medical research, right? You just need a different way to look at it. And the money rolls in without anyone getting hurt.* But maybe it's time to move on, the man reconsidered. It was heating up, and this business might bring him real trouble soon. *It would be better to explore some alternatives now, to work on my pain clinic thing and a few other ideas,* he decided, as he continued up I-95, making sure to keep well under the speed limit.

But the white-coated murderer hadn't been as alone and unseen as he'd thought. Georges Mondesir, the part-time orderly on the 8:00 p.m. to 4:00 a.m. shift, was completing his last task, loading and lining up the robot carts of medical equipment along the floor's darkened hallways for the next day's work. Georges got a kick out of the waist-high shiny white metal carts. With their metal poles extending necklike from the top tray, and their facelike computer screens lit up with electronic gobbledygook bleeping out digitized sounds, they seemed like little gnomes propelling themselves politely along the corridors, turning corners without bumping into anybody. *We're all night workers,* he reflected. *Nobody gives us a second thought, but the hospital couldn't do what it does without us.*

Georges never wanted anyone to think he was shirking his duties, so he was always careful not to head for the locker room until exactly the end of his shift. He glanced casually at his watch. *Still a few minutes to go.* He walked one last time down the row of carts, scanning the hallway as he strode along. He was startled to see a man in a white coat ahead of him, walking slowly, dragging his right leg, checking patient doorplates for names. The guy opened a room door and closed it behind him. *What the hell was that all about?* Georges asked himself. He'd worked this beat a little while and never saw any medical action this time of night, unless there was an emergency code and then the lights glared on and the floor became alive with nurses, aides, and so on. But now the hall was still silent, just this guy wearing a white coat. *That meant a doctor, didn't it? Everyone working at the hospital had a color that showed what job they did, white for doctors, who wore suits underneath . . . but, what the hey, I suppose anyone could pick up a white coat. . . .* He wondered if he should go down to the room, maybe crack open the door, and see what was going on. *But what if it is a doctor doing some medical stuff with a patient? I wouldn't be thanked for interfering. Some of these doctors are damned autocratic.* He couldn't afford to mess up, so he thought maybe it was better to mind his own business. He pushed off to the locker room, in the opposite direction, before the man came out of the room.

Georges hurried out of the building still in his green uniform, eager to catch his ride, a deal he'd arranged with a neighborhood gypsy cab driver. He'd be back in his rented room in Little Haiti by 4:30 a.m. This being Miami, there was practically no public transportation for working folks, and he couldn't take a chance with his bike at this time of the night—too dangerous. He had too much going for him now to risk lost workdays due to a mugging. He was lucky to have the job. Even the hours were a blessing, allowing him to attend college during the day. He thought with gratitude of his grandmother up north in Boca, their terrifying trip from Haiti to Florida when he was so young it was only a dim memory. Through her stories his grandmother kept his mom and dad alive for him. They had died, like so many others, in the Haitian dictatorship. She spoke Creole to him, told him about the gods of Haiti's vodou religion who would watch over them in the new land. He didn't know if he believed it all, but he promised himself he would visit Haiti some day and check it out for himself. Like many Haitians, his grandma signed on as a home health aide, working crazy hours so she could watch over him as he grew up and doing whatever was necessary for them to survive. She made sure he did well in school and learned perfect English.

Yeah, so grateful now, but he'd gone through a bad stretch as a teenager, hanging out, giving her grief, getting into fights all the time. Then he got a break. A Boca cop who'd pulled him out of a street brawl told him, "If you're so good with your fists, why don't you put them to real use and learn how to box?" The idea sounded exciting, glamorous. Even his grandmother approved, though she'd hoped he'd go in for a college-type sport like basketball or football that would earn him a scholarship later. But boxing was better than nothing. At least he'd be at a gym after school, supervised.

So Georges' soft Creole *g*'s became *j*'s, as he himself became Georgie, American style. He loved the boxing from the get-go, practiced like hell, and won a few local bouts, then a county title, and later a state championship. The other kids at the gym envied him his belts and his trophies. Some of his street buddies even followed him into the Police Athletic League (PAL) gym. His grandma filled scrapbooks with his newspaper clippings. Even his grades went up. *And the travel—staying in hotels and eating at fancy restaurants—was so cool.* He remembered how nervous he was at first. He felt proud, like the rich people he met, but also unsure, of which fork to use and what to do when his napkin fell on the floor. But still, his grandma's cooking was the best: *you couldn't beat her calalou, and none of those fancy desserts could match her pain patate.*

Still, the most important thing he'd learned wasn't throwing a lethal left hook; it was that you couldn't succeed—not in boxing and not in life—without dedication and hard work. He surprised himself by learning to respect some cops—the volunteers at the PAL gym and others who worked in different sports with the neighborhood kids—a respect he could never have imagined. He'd despised white folks for their arrogance, wealth, and hatred of the Haitians, but some of them were okay. Like Ric and Tommy, who really cared about him. Through the PAL, they arranged a scholarship at the top private school in South Florida. He'd jumped at it, did really well, and now look at him! He had a scholarship to the university, and this part-time gig at North Miami General that Tommy had connected him to earned him a few dollars so he could free up his grannie a bit. He lived with a Haitian family that looked out for him. He rationalized not blowing the whistle on the incident he'd just seen in the hospital: *Georges, my man, you got things just where they should be. Let the guys who get paid for it do the heavy lifting.* Then he amended, *Well, maybe on my next shift I'll ask around.*

January 1, 2009, 7:00 a.m.

"Dead!" The voice cried into the phone. "How can he be dead? His doctor said he was doing okay, even if he was in a coma. This is supposed to be a first-class hospital. How could this happen?"

The receptionist at the nurses' station clucked sympathetically. "Judging the condition of an elderly person is difficult," she began.

Another speaker crowded the receiver, interrupting her, "He wasn't elderly, fifty's not elderly."

"Well, but there were complications," the receptionist continued. "The deceased was discovered early this morning when rounds started. He just seemed to be sleeping peacefully, and perhaps that's the best way, isn't it?"

"Who are you to judge that?" the second voice took over the receiver. "We'll have a lot of questions to ask the doctor, you can bet."

"Of course, that's your right. I notice there's no funeral home listed on the contact sheet. Would you like us to suggest one? We often work with Comfort Providers; it's nearby and is quite reasonable and has an excellent reputation."

"Hold on a minute," requested the voice, returning to the phone in a few moments. "That sounds all right. We don't live in Florida, and it'll take us a few days to come down. There's no other close family. When can we speak to the doctor?"

"Well, today is New Year's Day. The doctor won't be in again until tomorrow," the receptionist responded without inflection. "I will leave a message that you want an appointment and have him call you." She paused. "We're very sorry for your loss."

"You just tell that doc we're gonna want some answers," the surly man's voice yelled into the phone before banging down the receiver.

🌴 Chapter Two

January 1, 2009, 7:30 a.m.

Julie Norman, a newly minted associate professor in cultural anthropology at NUNY, the New University of New York, settled down at her desk at home with her cappuccino, a new calendar, and a legal pad in front of her. She'd already washed and blow-dried her thick, glossy chestnut hair, which had grown long again after she'd cut it short for a donation to Women's Cancer Care. Her midnight black cat, Chairman Miao, leapt up and nestled comfortably in her lap, and began his soothing purr. Julie always made New Year's Day special, pursuing only pleasant activities, calling only people she loved or liked, and *not*, repeat *not*, engaging in any of the tedious, aggravating chores that now, as always, awaited her on the to-do list near her phone.

Her New Year's Eve dinner with her detective boyfriend Mike had been cut short by the ringing of his cell, a not unusual occurrence, but that was okay. Tonight, no matter what, they were attending the annual gala performance of *Revelations*, the joyous Alvin Ailey ballet steeped in black history and music. Her new slim-fitting black pants and off-the-shoulder, hip-length cashmere sweater were laid out on her bed. She'd add the long strand of her grandmother's Austrian crystal beads and wear her chic midlength leather boots that brought her to just the right height for Mike's

six-foot frame. She had a lot to celebrate. Her just-published book on Indian marriage and the family was garnering some good reviews, and her
promotion would bring both financial and professional perks in the new
year. Despite the claim of large public universities like NUNY that teaching was their primary mission, scholarly research and publication were still
the chief criteria for promotion. Now, after years of fieldwork in India, she
was ready to cast around for a new research area that would interest her
publisher, her students, and herself.

Last week Julie had called her Aunt Lottie in Florida to wish her Happy
New Year. She knew her aunt would probably be up early sitting at the
small, worn, Formica table in her cramped kitchen, watching her tiny
black-and-white TV set. She'd be drinking her instant coffee—"good
enough for me," she'd assert—and savoring one of those sugar-topped
supermarket donuts that Julie's mom swore would put her older sister
into an early grave. *Too late for that,* Julie had thought, as, grinning, she
had tapped in Aunt Lottie's phone number. Though older than Julie's
mom by twenty years, Lottie was a hearty soul, still trim despite her
eighty-some years, with the smoothest skin Julie had ever seen on an
elderly person. Despite two heart surgeries, her aunt was still basically in
good health. "I'll live to see you married, yet, Julie," she'd tell her niece
on every visit. "Maybe I won't be able to *dance* at your wedding"—a
reference to her arthritic feet that she encased in the most attractive "old
lady shoes" she could find—"but I'll certainly eat my share of the wedding cake. You know I'm still saving my diamond heart for you." *This
time,* Julie had considered, *when I go through the ritual of trying on the
diamond heart that Aunt Lottie wore at her own wedding, I'll drop a hint
that the longed-for day is at least a possibility.*

After her Uncle Sol had died, Julie had started telephoning her widowed
aunt weekly, taking her at her word that calling before 8:00 a.m. was fine.
"You can never call too early for me," Lottie had dismissed Julie's apolo-
gies. "We seniors don't sleep too well. What's an old lady like me got better
to do at six in the morning than talk with her favorite niece?" Lottie had
put herself on the nearby precinct's telephone service Senior Watch and

would joke to Julie that, when Officer Diaz-Woodson phoned, she enjoyed relating that her niece had beat her to the call again. Sometimes Lottie pooh-poohed the notion that the policewoman had to check with her every day, but Julie knew that her aunt enjoyed the expression of concern and her status as the officer's earliest "client." "Save the later hours for the lazybones," Aunt Lottie had advised the young officer, and occasionally the two of them took advantage of the quiet time for a brief chat.

Julie had confirmed to her aunt that she'd be down January 4th and spend the rest of the month with her. She'd rent a car, of course; America's car culture reached its epitome in Miami and along Florida's Gold Coast, and Julie would find it impossible to use public transportation for her outings with her aunt. "And I *might* have some news you'd like to hear." Julie couldn't finish her sentence before Aunt Lottie interrupted, excitement in her voice. "You met a fella; it's serious, right? Tell me I'm right." Not answering her question directly, Julie had just smiled a little to herself and said, "Aunt Lottie, we'll have all of January to talk. Be well. I'll see you soon."

Now, Julie gently tumbled Chairman Miao off her lap and started putting together her stuff for Florida. She stacked a sheaf of articles she'd collected on some new art galleries and restaurants in the Miami area, noting how chic and lively Miami and Miami Beach had become each time she visited. A special treat would be the mid-January South Beach Art Deco weekend, with parades and related events along the beachfront and Collins Avenue. If the weather was bad, she'd take Aunt Lottie to the huge indoor malls that offered galleries, cafés, and occasionally midday entertainment in addition to department stores and boutiques. Her aunt never tired of meandering through the department store aisles, even though she hardly ever bought anything. "I've got enough Hadassah outfits to last me another lifetime," she'd tell Julie, referring to her closetful of matched pantsuits in a rainbow of Florida pastels that she wore to her luncheons supporting the Jewish charity. On her visits, Julie always left a sizeable check for the group, which Aunt Lottie repeatedly reminded her had the best hospitals in the world and that "they treat everybody alike, Arabs, Jews, whatever, running to every earthquake and tsunami with their doctors and nurses."

Although Julie was always somewhat saddened by the knots of elderly women—and sprinkling of men—with their walkers, wheelchairs, and canes—who lined the benches in the mall, the scene didn't seem to faze Aunt Lottie. *She knows she'll be there someday*, Julie had figured out, *but what's the point of spoiling her enjoyment of the moment*. By 3:00 or 4:00 p.m., when the high school kids invaded, Aunt Lottie would nudge Julie to go back to the car, and they would decide on which restaurant to make for the early bird dinner. They'd be home again for the evening news, which Aunt Lottie took very seriously and liked to comment on to Julie as they had a last cup of tea. *Another perfect day*, her aunt would think to herself as she hugged Julie in a gesture that was as welcome as it was infrequent— neither she nor Julie's own mom were big huggers.

Julie usually managed a weeklong visit to her aunt at least once a year, but in the last year or so, Julie had felt the brevity of these visits was disappointing to Lottie. "Always in such a rush," her aunt would say plaintively, expressing loneliness and even discontent with her life in the apartment complex she and Sol had retired to many years ago. *Their move to Florida was halfway between the American Dream and an American Tragedy*, Julie often reflected. Only after their son Bobby had died of an overdose as a casualty of the heavy Bronx drug scene had they decided to move to South Florida to *try* to get some pleasure in their "golden years," as Lottie sarcastically phrased it. The loss of their only child, which foreclosed the joy of future grandchildren, never really went away, but they had made the best of their decision.

Their complex in North Miami was not a formal retirement community but rather a series of three-story-high rental buildings that formed an ersatz neighborhood of people similar to themselves, mostly Jewish or Italian, from various midwestern cities with cold climates. Apart from a few single women or widows, most were couples who'd raised their children to positions of financial security—"more or less," Aunt Lottie would tell Julie, swaying her hand up and down in their gossip sessions about the neighbors. "Lots of them exaggerate." Julie laughed in agreement; she knew loads of jokes about that aspect of South Florida culture. While the area had no lively streets to walk, there was a mall a few blocks away where Aunt Lottie could reinstitute her weekly Friday ritual at the beauty parlor, gossiping with her hairdresser and manicurist. She would shop by herself at the large Publix, not one of the fancy new supermarkets like those in the more upscale neighborhoods, but good enough for Lottie and Sol and their neighbors, who had saved enough to retire "with a few bucks left over," as they said in their friendly but deliberately vague fashion. The new Hadassah chapter Lottie had joined included many members who drove and were glad to pick her up for functions. "Not for nothing, understand," Lottie had repeated to Julie in more recent years. "Let's face it, these days new members for Hadassah don't fall out of the palm trees." When Julie regaled her mother, an English professor at another NUNY branch, with this vividly mixed metaphor, her mom immediately tried it out: "Let's face it, Dean Fabiolo, these days new students for liberal arts don't fall out of the sycamores." They'd both laughed so hard they almost fell off their chairs. They vowed they would find at least one professional meeting a year where they would put it to use.

Between Sol's insurance policy and Aunt Lottie's pension as the head bookkeeper in a large New York City hardware store, they were easily able to afford tickets for the downtown musicals and Miami Beach hotel entertainments for which a bunch of neighbors would chip in to rent a bus. With Bobby gone, her aunt and uncle could travel as they never had in the days when they feared every telephone call would bring a fresh disaster, and they ventured about on cruises and guided tours to Europe and Israel. Expensive opera glasses she had bought for her new life were now part of Lottie's treasured inheritance for Julie: "when I die," she'd say, she and Julie spitting three times through their fingers to ward off bad luck.

Lottie's clique formed a lobby-sitting audience for the handsome, tanned young mailman who told them risqué old folks jokes, gratefully accepted their lemonade and home-baked cookies, and chortled that he had the best job in America. The "girls" made up a Thursday night canasta group, with a few "alternates"—"just like a jury," Aunt Lottie quipped— who sat in when various members were away on trips or visiting their children. Sol and his cronies held frequent pinochle games under the big striped sun umbrellas alongside the pool, where no one swam except visiting grandkids, when the men would move the table farther back so the noisy splashing children didn't disrupt their game or spritz the cards. Sol's best friend, Lou, a somewhat younger single pharmacist living with his aged mother, had introduced him to the dog races and jai alai, where Lou would "bet a bundle," as Sol termed it, while he himself just gambled a token amount for the fun of it.

In the last decade, though, her aunt's neighborhood had become run down and more heavily immigrant, filling with Cubans and other Latin American ethnicities, too, who seemed increasingly impoverished with each year. The local mall closed its Publix, many of the better department stores moved away, and the teenagers from the local high school seemed more raucous and even more threatening than formerly. The original couples were increasingly widows or widowers, but the surviving spouses remained, lamenting, "Where are we going to go?" Moving back up north to live with their children was out of the question. They had totally bought into the American culture of aging with dignity and independence to the highest possible degree; it was an essential part of their self-respect. So they stayed on, an ever more diminished and isolated community, their comfort zones narrowing, attached to the larger life outside the complex mostly by the umbilical cord of those neighbors who ferried them to the upscale Aventura Mall a half-hour away or to their doctors' offices nearby.

Lou, nicknamed "the saint" by Aunt Lottie's clique, would sometimes do the supermarket shopping for the frailer women or pick up their visiting relatives at the airport and chauffeur them back again. When Sol had died, Lou had gone out of his way for Lottie, most importantly arranging for her to hire Charlotte, his own mother's capable and reliable Jamaican caregiver whom Lottie knew well, for 9:00 a.m. to 6:00 p.m. weekday shifts, before anyone else could grab her. But lately, in Julie's phone calls, Lou was only "the so-called saint" whose Vegas gambling trips took up more of his time. "He's off gallivanting more and not so good-hearted like he was," Lottie would tell Julie. "Okay, he'll still do some of my shopping if Charlotte can't get the car one day, but he doesn't pick the fruit so carefully as he used to—remember last year when I told him you were coming down? You see what he bought. The bananas looked good on the outside, but they were already mushy—I could tell he really didn't feel them—and the peaches were hard as rocks. Now he pays much more attention to Betty, and she has a son, even if he's in Ohio, who owns his own business and can come down whenever he wants, but I have nobody. When we all chipped in last year to buy Lou a shirt for his birthday, I put in the most money, but he treated the other girls much better than me."

Since two of Lottie's best friends had recently died—unexpectedly, with nobody really understanding the exact cause of their deaths—and Lottie had quarreled with a couple of her original card-playing neighbors, she groused to Julie that she couldn't even keep up a canasta game anymore. Julie had listened with some sympathy, but she'd felt a little insulted that Aunt Lottie had said "I have nobody" right to her face. Julie knew that, compared to some of her friends with less excuse, she saw more of her aunt than they did of their close-by elderly relatives. "I have no one to really talk to anymore," Lottie kept repeating, oblivious to Julie's feelings. "Even at the incinerator, nobody can say 'hello' in English except the school children . . . not that I have anything against Cubans," she assured Julie hastily. "Everybody comes here for the American Dream, right? They work hard, but they're so different from us—Spanish all the time, their loud music out by the pool even late at night, young people and old people and babies all in the same apartment, coming and going at all hours, good natured, you know, but just not like it used to be."

Julie had to acknowledge the demographic change. The emptying apartments *were* filling with Cubans, or other Spanish speakers, most of whom could not in fact speak enough English to help Aunt Lottie if she'd needed it. Julie's mom had suggested her sister move back up to New York to a "residencia," a hybrid type of independent living complex that was becoming popular, and then they could visit her more often. "Out of the question," Aunt Lottie was adamant. "The weather would kill me, and there's nobody left in the Bronx anymore. And all the doctors are down here."

"Yeah, yeah," Julie's mom had rebutted. "Only several million nobodies in the Bronx and what doctor could compare to that pompous Galbinki with his gushy receptionist and homemade testimonials all over his wall. His office looks like a kindergarten bulletin board on Valentine's Day," Julie's mom ran on with her typical sarcastic humor. But they both knew Lottie's arguments were reasonable. *Maybe on this trip*, Julie thought, *I'll start looking for a Gold Coast alternative for her.*

🌴 Chapter Three

Before leaving for Florida, Julie visited her neighborhood public library to check out some books for her vacation. As she came out, she ran into Fatima, a new anthropology colleague in her department, with whom she shared a common interest in gender issues and south Asian cultures. Julie had taken Fatima under her wing, as the young woman had just moved to New York from the small town in Iowa where she had been a student, and she was still a little bewildered by the unwritten rules and culture of both NUNY and the big city.

After exchanging hugs, Julie stepped back and looked intently at Fatima. "You look a little troubled," she said. "Is everything okay?"

Fatima hesitated, then asked Julie, "Is there any chance you have time for a coffee? I have a kind of personal problem—nothing to do with school, but I think it would be helpful for me to talk with you about it."

"No problem," Julie replied. "There's a coffee and bagel place right around the corner. I think you just moved into Chelsea, didn't you?"

"Yes, I did," Fatima answered as they settled into a booth in the nearly empty shop. "I was so lucky to get an apartment around here. If it weren't for the economic downturn, I could never have afforded such a nice place. It's only a studio, but it suits me perfectly, and the location is most convenient." After a short silence and a few sips of coffee, Julie looked directly at her friend. "So tell me, what's on your mind? I'll be happy to help if I can."

"It's not so much help I need as maybe some advice or encouragement to do what I need to do. You know in our Muslim culture, the Koran obliges us to care for our elderly relatives at home, and we do want to do that. Even we modern immigrants to America take that obligation very seriously. But the realities of our lives often make that difficult, if not impossible. My mom is getting on in years and unfortunately is ill as well. My dad died a couple of years ago and I'm the only child here. My brother works for a multinational in Japan and he travels all the time. He can't really take care of Mom, and in any case, she'd never move to such a foreign culture as Japan. She lived with me when I went to college, and I thought she could join me here in New York, but I have such a small apartment, and I can't afford anything bigger. I guess maybe if I moved out to Queens or the suburbs I could afford a larger place, but right now I have to put my time into my teaching and my research, and do well, you know? I'm going crazy over what is the right thing to do. As a Muslim daughter, the idea of putting my mom into a nursing home, even temporarily, is utterly unthinkable."

As tears welled up in Fatima's eyes, Julie reached over for her hand. "You're right, Fatima, you really are in a difficult situation. It's part of what America offers and at the same time takes away. It used to be mainly men who had to move out to move up, but now women are experiencing that as well. We want to better ourselves professionally, but that often requires us to relocate and leave our parents behind in a different place. You know, it's 'the good news is, I got a great job, the bad news is, it's out in North Dakota—or somewhere.' I've been having similar thoughts myself. I'm leaving in a couple of days to stay with my elderly aunt in Florida; she's a widow now with no close relatives down there. My mom and I are her closest family, but we'd never think of moving down there. And by this time, she really couldn't move back to New York either. I'm thinking maybe I can just get her into a different situation in Florida. The place where she lives now is getting run down and isn't really safe any more.

"Of course, it's different for us Americans. With all kinds of suitable retirement communities, assisted-living facilities, and even good nursing homes in Florida, there are some acceptable alternatives. These have actually become part of American culture. However much we genuinely care about our elderly relatives, our lives here are just not set up to provide for ill or fragile older parents in our homes. You know, the Italians have a saying, 'When the parents give to their child, the parents laugh and the child laughs, but when the child gives to the parents, the child cries and the parents cry.' It's all about our traditional Western ideal of independence, caring for ourselves. I do understand that it's different for you."

"I know that, Julie. I suppose that's what anthropology teaches us. But it's different when you have to adapt in your own life. Then it's not a theory, but a reality, and you have to come to terms with it. I just don't know what I can do."

"Actually, Fatima, I do have one idea you might think about," Julie offered. "I read an article in the *Times* last week, in fact I saved it; it was so anthropological. It was about Muslim working families that have to consider options for their elderly relatives outside the home. It happens here more than you think. So some Muslim Americans got together to design assisted-living and nursing home facilities that would make these options more acceptable. They're building these living spaces adjoining mosques, or providing communal prayer rooms where there are several Muslim clients and they can serve halal food and offer same-sex medical care that would suit these older folks. They try to get multilingual staff members who can help these elderly people feel more comfortable in their new environment. The article listed some resources that you might explore; see if anything works for you. When I come back from Florida, I'll look around with you if you like. Of course, none of these facilities are in Manhattan yet, but I have some contacts in Brooklyn where I did some political outreach and maybe they could help you. Or perhaps an imam in some neighborhood mosque. It's a start, anyway."

Fatima brightened up and smiled at Julie. "Oh, Julie," she said. "How lucky I am to have you for a friend. I'll let you go on your way now and will follow up on your suggestions. When you return, I will let you know what I have learned. Do have a good vacation, and best wishes for your aunt. She is lucky to have such a niece as you."

As Julie left to continue her last-minute errands, she reflected on her conversation with Fatima and on the lifestyle changes for the elderly even in supposed paradises like Florida. Yes, the promise there was rich, but—except for the privileged winners with extensive financial resources and excellent genes—aging, dying, and death were, as Aunt Lottie would put it, "no picnic." Ironically, Julie reminded herself, the "natural" links most Americans intuited between old age and death were not universal. In poor countries, or those torn apart by horrific wars, death was associated with children and young men and women. In many of those places, people didn't live long enough to experience debilitating diseases like Alzheimer's or cancer. In other cultures, at least formerly, before the spread of modern medical technologies, adult children rarely had the problems of the American "sandwich generation" with their financial worries about the kids' college tuition while simultaneously facing the burden of care for aged parents, whose physical lives had been extended for many years beyond their mobility or mental capacity.

As Julie mulled over her Aunt Lottie's situation, she thought about the culture of aging, which, she knew, was different in different places. In America, it was all about not being a burden on your children but instead basking in the reflected glory of their accomplishments and those of your grandchildren. As Fatima's conversation had indicated, and as she knew from conversations with Kwame, her good friend and NUNY colleague, aging in America was very different from aging elsewhere, such as in the Ghanaian village where Kwame had grown up. His deep concerns for family relationships always elicited a nod of understanding when Julie outlined some of the difficulties involved in her relationship with her aunt.

"We must always take care of the elders," he would say, "and never forget our ancestors—the living *and* the dead. In my culture it is our first priority. Our elders have taken care of us and now in their old age we must reciprocate. And it is not a one-way street, Julie. Our ancestors are much wiser than us and can advise us in useful ways to help us in our own lives." Julie doubted whether the authority accorded to the elders and, even more so, the ancestors held true in most mainstream American families. She remembered an advertisement she had seen for a storage place recently: "If you store your stuff at your parents' house, you have to visit." Kwame, Fatima, and probably traditional African Americans and first-generation immigrant families from Africa, Latin America, and Asia would find that appalling, if they could even understand it. Focusing on the old simply was not a core value for middle-class whites, whose educated adult children and especially their grandchildren had grown up with the notion that technology could solve all problems. It was these technologically savvy generations who had grown up with computers, cell phones, BlackBerries, iPods, Bluetooths, and so on, who possessed the life skills to succeed in the contemporary world and not their "ancestors," to many of whom these tech toys were a mystery. *This is a generation gap like no other*, Julie considered, thinking of her own mom, brilliant and self-sufficient in so many ways but almost a technological luddite. Even Kai, her mom's beloved seven-year-old grandson, was critical of her technological gaps, which included, in his case, complete ignorance about how to manipulate his robotic superheroes. "You got to use this stuff, Grandma," he'd say, his little round face crinkled in concern when he showed her some new tech toy or computer device he'd learned to use. "It's not too hard. I can teach you some simple things, and it's lots of fun."

Smiling to herself as she thought about these encounters, Julie's ruminations moved to the currently expanded interest in the anthropology of aging. Like every biological aspect of being human, the experience of growing older was shaped by cultural meanings and social institutions. For most Americans, that meant looking at aging primarily through a biological lens, where it was depressingly linked to physical deterioration, a decline in sexual appeal and vigor, and a prelude to death. While in other, more traditional cultures, old age had its own stand-alone positive meanings that required no apology or denial, Americans largely found that the solution for getting old was to become younger. The booming commercial antiaging market—Botox, cosmetic surgery, even "rejuvenating toothpaste"—marked, and marketed, old age as an unambiguous negative, something to deny, hold off, and prevent. *But those perceptions aren't static*, Julie amended. *They can be and are being influenced by competing cultural factors. New emphases on nutrition, exercise, antistress activities, and even a shift in values are all having an impact.* Despite all the youth-oriented advertising hoping to make old people feel bad about themselves and buy products, and even with the restrictions imposed by the ideal of the one-generation nuclear family and the real physical limitations accompanying old age, the senior years were gaining traction, Julie thought. A poll she'd recently read seemed to indicate that many senior citizens were fairly happy with their lives, although it was clear that that outcome was weighted toward those with better health and bigger bucks. *Would it be the same now*, Julie wondered, *with pensions, 401(k)s, and jobs in the toilet?*

Economics play such an important cultural role everywhere, she thought. She perfectly recalled how her students had shuddered at a film explaining the Inuit custom of leaving their elderly out on an ice floe when they became economic burdens. But hadn't she just shuddered over a newspaper account of a woman who had lost her job and then abandoned her elderly father in his wheelchair at a football game because she could no longer afford to care for him? In today's rapidly globalizing world, Julie knew better than to romanticize aging even in more traditional societies. Those societies might still respect age as an ideal, but in reality that respect also depended on whether the elders still controlled important resources or had many dependents who could extend their influence in their society. Almost everywhere now, the experience of growing old and the treatment of the elderly depended largely on their ability to function productively and add to, not diminish, the resources to care for them. Many cultures were being driven to find harsh solutions to difficult problems.

Even in countries like India, which put great emphasis on respect and care for the elderly, Julie's fieldwork had illustrated the current complexity of the issue. Despite its rapid economic modernization, India was still trying its best to hold on to its traditional family values. During her extensive participant-observation research there, she'd met several families where an elderly grandparent was living with a son and his family, even in fairly impoverished conditions. She'd found several three-generation households that did seem genuinely at ease with the situation. She recalled one urban tenement she'd visited, where the frail old grandmother appeared to be a truly valued center of family life, even though she was too physically incapacitated to help out in the home and, in fact, needed a great deal of care herself. Yet the teenaged granddaughter and her kindergarten-aged sibling appeared to be totally unresentful in fulfilling their small tasks for her, and it was true that her mere presence in the house allowed both parents to work.

Yet Julie could see that many Indians *had* had to make adjustments to modern conditions regarding their grandparent generation. Many sons did try to continue the Indian patrilineal extended family system, where a son's duty to care for his aged parents was a given. But today's ambitious sons, seeking to join the competitive global march, often had to move far away from their parents, sometimes to other continents. The patrilineal family *was* beginning to fray, and while dutiful emigrant children still sent money back to their families, that wasn't the same thing as being there. And for the older family patriarch, being on the receiving end of financial resources unavoidably weakened his central position in the family. Even nursing homes were opening in India because of the changing demographics. *No easy solutions*, thought Julie. *Everyone applauds medical advances, but longer life also means more years of physical decline and decreasing productive participation in society, just when material resources are becoming scarcer.*

Julie pondered China, too, another nation where the ancient value of caring for the aged at home was being altered. With young folk rushing to the cities to take part in the economic boom, the old folk were left with the grandchildren in the villages. This reality was undercutting the traditional Confucian obligations for a son to provide for his aged parents. She'd read that, in some urban communities, local neighborhood committees were publicly posting the names of adult children who neglected their elderly parents in an effort to shame them, and some institutional homes for the elderly—previously unheard of—were fining children who missed their weekend parental visits. The only upside here was that, as daughters were becoming more reliable than sons in this respect, the Chinese cultural preference for boys was slowly giving way. *Fatima's dilemma—a good anthropological theme—illustrates how basic economics led toward cultural convergence.*

But some societies appear to have escaped the gap between their ideals and current economic realities, Julie reconsidered. According to her reading about the Ju/'hoansi of Botswana, a society made famous by the ethnography of Richard Lee in the 1960s, this resource-poor, supposedly primitive group was able to retain intact their traditional ideology of sharing as an integral part of their subsistence hunting-and-gathering economy. The Ju/'hoansi did not consider the elders a burden, even those who couldn't care for themselves. And the difficulties of old age, including the decline of sexual prowess—but not sexual interest—among both men and women, was a source of Ju/'hoansi humor. *Would the Ju/'hoansi men use Viagra if they could get it,* Julie wondered, *or would aging Ju/'hoansi women support a billion-dollar youth-enhancing industry with tummy tucks and face lifts?* Julie didn't think so, but if the money and services were available, who knew? Ju/'hoansi elders valued their independence and autonomy, and those who could participated in economic activities, were socially active, made crafts, and danced and performed essential healing ceremonies as long as they could. According to the literature, they didn't appear frightened of being poor or express anxiety about their personal security. They seemed to retain confidence that their community would remain responsible for them. They had no history of interpersonal violence or abuse, loneliness, or abandonment by their families to factor into their assumptions about their later years. Was that because, unlike in America, they had no private property to pass on, so there was no reason for them to become targets of malice or even murder, from relatives or others in a position to exploit them? *But in a future where the community might prosper economically and individuals would begin to amass private property—especially livestock— would all that change?* Julie wondered. As she meditated on these issues, Julie again thought of Aunt Lottie and how they would need to explore all of the issues—emotional and financial—before she made the next big move in her life.

When Julie's cell rang, she offhandedly picked it up, supposing it was either Mike—surprisingly early—or her mom. But to her surprise, it was Aunt Lottie's normally unflappable caregiver, Charlotte, speaking now with some anxiety.

"Hello, Julie, I don't want to worry you, but last night I had to take your aunt to the emergency room. Lou was out of town so she called me; she said she was having heart palpitations, a rapid heartbeat, and her face was flushing, maybe from her high blood pressure. Fortunately, I was up watching the New Year's Eve fireworks. She didn't want an ambulance, just asked me to rush her over to North Miami General and wait 'til she was settled in a room. Dr. Galbinki called me this morning. He saw her already and thinks it's just that arrhythmia, like the palpitations she'd had a couple of times before. He'll keep her about a week, doing different tests, and he'll call me every day until you get down. Of course, if you aren't down by the time she's dismissed . . ."

"Not to worry, Charlotte," Julie said. "My plane gets in the afternoon of the fourth, and I'm renting a car. I'll go straight to the hospital. We can take her home together whenever she's ready."

"Oh, I'm much relieved, Julie. I did call the Senior Watch to alert them she wouldn't be answering her phone for a few days. That officer Diaz-Woodson was very nice and said she'd stop by to visit your aunt in the hospital. Me or one of my children will stop by every day too. I'm glad you're coming down soon, though." As Charlotte's voice trailed off, Julie assured her again she'd go to the hospital as soon as she landed. "Maybe I can even catch Galbinki that night. I know these doctors attend their patients either very early or very late, and I'm determined to see him."

Julie knew that Charlotte, like herself, wasn't a fan of Aunt Lottie's favorite doctor. While Julie didn't agree with her mom that he was a *fake*— although Florida had more unlicensed physicians than any other state in the union—the *pompous* part was right on, in her view. Or at best, Galbinki was yet another *condescending* friend of the elderly. He'd never called her Dr. Norman, even when she introduced herself with her title, finally snapping at her, "But you're not a doctor of medicine, are you?" *No*, Julie had fumed to herself, *but barbers used to do medicine, and even the biggest physicians in England are called just plain Mister.*

🌴 Chapter Four

Julie completed her family phone calls, ringing up her mom, another early riser, and her sister Jennie's family, wishing her and Dave and little Kai a Happy New Year. She e-mailed some dear friends and colleagues around the world and, later in the day, confirmed with her friend Pauli that he should be at her apartment on the third to start taking care of Chairman Miao. Pauli, a dancer and actor whose lively aerobic classes Julie had taken for years, had his own co-op in Brooklyn's Sheepshead Bay, thanks to Julie's networking with a Russian friend. But he was always delighted with his vacations at her Chelsea apartment in the heart of Manhattan's gay scene, where he was also closer to his theater-district auditions. He was okay with Julie's "no visitors" policy and lovingly cared for her little terrace garden, often adding fresh herbs, orchids, and seasonal flowers from the city's plant district only a few blocks away. When Julie returned from her trips, a spike of accurately dated phone messages sat on her desk, and the fridge was filled with unfinished bottles of wine and single-portion containers of his Italian mother's homemade lasagna.

Julie's flight landed at Miami airport just a little after 2:00 p.m., into cold and rainy weather as expected. By the time she retrieved her bag from the

carousel, hopped on the correct rental-car bus at the airport's exit, and
finished her business at the understaffed counters of the car agency, the
rain had become a downpour and the sky was thunderously dark. When
the baseball-capped dispatcher pointed to a compact in the second row,
she fled the flimsy shelter of the torn cloth awning, thrust the keys into the
vehicle, and flung open the door, wriggling out of her soaked coat.

The receipt in the glove compartment told her the car was a Korean
KIA. *An unpropitious name,* she thought. *Aren't the Koreans supposed to be
savvy marketers?* But there was no manual. As she struggled with the dash
indicators to find the lights, the wipers, and the heat, she was dismayed
to see there was no GPS screen. Though Miami was no longer the car-
jacking capital it had once been, and the hospital was not far from Lottie's
apartment, Julie now had only a vague recall of the route. She couldn't
remember which exit number to take off I-95, where the traffic was whiz-
zing by her unmercifully in what was now total darkness. Taking a chance
on the next exit, she found herself on totally unfamiliar, barely illuminated
streets in what looked like the area in which there'd been a recent capture
of a houseful of terrorist wannabes. There wasn't a soul around to give her
directions, but she sighed with relief at spotting a lighted corner gas station.
Then she sunk disgustedly in her seat as she realized that the proliferation
of "pump your own" stations had emptied this area, like so much of Miami
in the eighties, of the gas jockey, patron saint of the lost motorist. Grimly,
Julie U-turned to drive away when she spotted a car backing out behind
the tiny station store. Beeping her horn and flapping her free hand wildly,
she drew the driver's attention. His lucid directions finally got her to the
hospital, but it took some driving down obscure streets before she hit the
main boulevard she needed, and she vowed that on her next trip down
she'd rise at 4:00 a.m. if necessary to take a flight that would *definitely* land
with plenty of daylight hours ahead.

Julie parked as close as she could to the hospital entrance but still got
soaked in her dash to the door. She shook off her coat and obtained the
number of her aunt's room from the receptionist. As she arrived on the
floor, she was taken aback by a shiny white metal cart about waist high,

holding various items of medical equipment on its open shelves, rolling down the corridor on its own. Magically avoiding Julie, who hugged the wall, the medical cart turned a corner on its own and entered an open doorway right next to her aunt's. "It's a hospital robot," a lilting Caribbean voice informed Julie as its owner followed her into Lottie's room. Julie tiptoed past the first bed, which held the sleeping form of an older woman, and drew the curtain fully around the second bed, by the window, where her aunt was sitting up against the pillows watching a TV without the sound.

"Oh, Aunt Lottie," Julie whispered, kissing her soft pink cheek, "Charlotte gave me quite a scare with her phone call. I'm happy to see you looking so well."

"Clarice," Lottie addressed the aide in the blue uniform through Julie's kiss. "This is my niece, Julie."

Julie waved and nodded, and Clarice turned cheerfully toward Lottie. "You'd never believe it, but this feisty ole lady is quite Mrs. Popularity, more visitors than the law allows. If she keeps it up, the Medicare will raise her rates." Aunt Lottie waved away the aide's words.

"Just that lovely Officer Diaz-Woodson and some Hadassah ladies, and of course, Charlotte and her son even came over, and Dr. Galbinki's here in the morning and at night. You just missed him, Julie; I know he'd like to see you." *Right! Like he'd enjoy a hungry alligator tearing at his Armani pants leg.* Julie just nodded pleasantly to her aunt. "I'm too tired now to even ask questions," she said, and added, "You must be tired, too."

"Not too tired for a little chat," her aunt said. "But we'll keep it down. Mrs. Greene in the next bed, she came in from the emergency room a couple of nights ago; she has some heart palpitations just like me. But she doesn't like the doctor they assigned her as much as she likes Dr. Galbinki. He always stops by to chat with her. She's a widow, too. She came down to visit her son and daughter-in-law, but they've hardly come to see her at all. I think maybe they don't get along too well. Not like me and my Julie," she smiled fondly at her niece. "She told me that since her husband passed away she comes down a few times a year from New York and sometimes takes one of those Caribbean cruises that leave from Miami. Her husband left her very well off, I think, and she sold their big house in Westchester after he died. Now she has one of those luxury apartments in Riverdale. She takes the express buses down to the city a lot to shop and go to the theatre . . . some of us old ladies do have a nice life despite our ills, isn't that so?" she mused.

Aunt Lottie interrupted herself to ask Clarice to turn off the television set. "Even without the sound, I can't stand to watch it. Horrible TV shows they have down here, you can't believe it, Julie, young girls on a stage with a bunch of different men, arguing about which one is the father of their child. To expose their problems like that in front of strangers? What are they thinking? I remember when our second cousin Betty got a divorce after she married that no-goodnik Herbie and we kept it a secret for years, it was considered such a shame." Julie agreed that times had indeed changed, *though maybe not all for the worse*, she amended silently. *Divorce isn't the worst outcome to a bad marriage*, she reflected, sadly recalling the murdered wife case that had introduced her to Mike the previous year. Wearing her anthropology hat, though, she credited her aunt with asking just the right question: *what kind of culture encouraged people to find such programs entertaining?*

"Now that's better," Lottie thanked Clarice as she shut off the TV. "Those robots'll never take away your job; the television sets are too high for them to reach." Lottie chortled at her own joke and then told Julie, "You know, Clarice is the only person on the whole floor besides that robot that shows up just when she's needed. The nurses are totally useless; they say 'wait just one minute,' and they're gone for hours. When I came in here, the nurse—a *pisher* that looked sixteen years old—she took away all my own clothes and my little makeup bag and buried it so deep it took Clarice a day to find it. I looked terrible when Dr. Galbinki came to see me; I couldn't even comb my hair. And she talked to me like I was too deaf or stupid to understand what was going on. 'I've been here for two heart surgeries,' I told her. 'I probably know as much as you do about how to treat a heart patient.' And some of the doctors, Julie, they're worse than that robot for bedside manners. The second day I'm here, the Sunday substitute doctor comes in all cheery, thinking of the fat fee he'll get just for stepping through the door . . . and I tell him I need to see my chart to make sure all the dosages for my different pills for my different conditions are right. He says, 'Everything's computerized now; there aren't any more charts, Mrs. Fried'"—Lottie interrupted her account to exclaim, "He didn't even have my correct name. Like the time Sol's doctor calls him secretly to come in so they could talk about his syphilis treatment and it turns out his receptionist—his wife, you see, to save money—she had mixed Sol's chart up with some other man's." Lottie paused a moment, then added, "Poor fellow." By now, Julie and Clarice were stifling their laughter with their hands so as not to disturb Mrs. Greene.

"So, I said," Lottie continued, "'Doctor, then you go right outside and bring me the computer printout.' See," she turned confidentially to Clarice for agreement, "he figured an old lady like me wouldn't know about computers. But he didn't know my niece is a professor who takes her laptop on every visit, right Julie?" Smiling slyly, Lottie continued with her saga. "'I'm not allowed to give you a printout,' this doctor continues. Of course, I know that; they're afraid I might sue the hospital if they made a mistake. Well, the next morning when Dr. Galbinki comes in, Julie, I'm telling you, he knows how to work with his patients; he says he'll get it for me and check it himself and let me look at it." She leaned back with satisfaction. "'But no taking notes' he warns me. See, Julie, they're *all* worried about lawsuits, even the good ones. Only Clarice doesn't treat me like a mental case or a child."

Clarice clucked her tongue, and Julie chuckled in her throat at her aunt's recital. "Your aunt does speak truth to power," said the aide as she lowered the bed into sleeping position and fluffed Lottie's pillows. "I won't stay long, Clarice," Julie said as she waved goodbye, "her eyes are closing already." Julie stayed only a few minutes more, assuring her aunt that she'd be back very early the next morning in order to catch Galbinki and get the details of Lottie's condition.

Chapter Five

The next morning Julie awoke refreshed and delighted to see blue sky, although the wind was still high. As she entered her aunt's hospital room she saw Dr. Galbinki just leaving. He didn't look as sharp as he usually did; there were bags under his eyes, and he seemed in a hurry to move on. *Give the guy credit*, Julie conceded, *he's probably been seeing his patients since sunrise.* Nevertheless, she politely but firmly blocked his way at the door.

"Yes? *Dr.* Norman," the physician asked with some asperity, emphasizing her title to let Julie know that he remembered their original encounter perfectly.

"I know how busy you are, Dr. Galbinki," Julie said in an ingratiating tone. "I just want an update on my aunt's condition." His smooth manner somewhat restored, he told Julie that his tests and examination showed that her aunt's rapid heart rate and flushed face had not indicated a serious attack and that he would just adjust her blood pressure medication and keep her in the hospital one more day. "You can take her home tomorrow afternoon if you have time . . . or, rather, if you can arrange it with Charlotte. She should probably pick her up in that big Buick of hers since you're probably driving a small rental car. That would be more comfortable for your aunt." *Did this guy have eyes in the back of his head?* Julie griped inwardly. *If he knew it was a KIA—he'd probably refuse to let her ride with me at all.* But Julie acknowledged his suggestion with enthusiasm, as if he hadn't meant to convey that she had just come down for sun and fun and was only squeezing in a few minutes with her old auntie so she'd be remembered in her will.

"Oh, Julie, I'm so glad you're here," her aunt said as her niece settled herself in the chair by the bed. "I didn't sleep at all well last night. It's so odd; in the middle of the night I thought I heard someone come in the door and stand by Mrs. Greene's bed behind the curtain. I could only see the curtain waving a little you know, but of course, I couldn't see who it was. Maybe I just dreamed the whole thing. I could hardly get back to sleep. She's such a nice woman. But this morning, when Clarice drew the curtain, I saw that her bed was empty. When I asked Clarice where she'd gone, I really didn't get a straight answer. I do hope the poor woman didn't pass away in the night."

"Now look, Aunt Lottie," Julie admonished. "Don't go worrying about such things. She's probably downstairs for tests or something, or maybe she's even been discharged by now."

"No," Lottie countered, "they don't discharge until after the lunch hour. I must ask Clarice again when she comes by. Now, why don't you go out and enjoy yourself for a while. Arlene and maybe Frankie, too, if he's up to it—he's been ill recently—are coming down to see me today. You know it's a long drive for them, and they like to stay a bit. They told me they're bringing a whole carton of food containers for me and they'll drop it off at my apartment so it won't defrost. They have my key, so you don't have to worry about staying home for them. But maybe you'll run into them; that would be nice." *Very nice,* Julie swallowed her true thoughts, *then I don't have to watch the Sopranos on TV for the next three days.*

"But do come back by five," her aunt continued. "Dr. Galbinki starts his evening rounds then and we want to be sure to catch him. I do so want to leave the hospital tomorrow." Julie nodded her assurance, kissed her aunt, and left the room, happy that she'd have some time to unpack and put her clothes away and figure out a plan for the month. She certainly didn't want to bump into Arlene and Frankie. She'd check out a nearby bird sanctuary she'd heard about and then return to the hospital after her aunt's visitors had gone.

When Julie returned to her aunt's room well before 5:00 p.m., her aunt was alone, the bed next to hers still empty. A huge bouquet of flowers graced her tray table—"from Arlene and Frankie, aren't they beautiful?" Her aunt smiled. "They're so thoughtful that way. Sit down, Julie, make yourself comfortable; I have a lot to tell you." Julie knew as much about Arlene and Frankie and their family as she wanted to, but she wouldn't spoil her aunt's fun in detailing her news. She knew the backstory from previous visits. Arlene, Sol's youngest sister, trim and attractive, had married Frankie in her early thirties. Frankie was quite a few years older than she but handsome and charming in the Italian manner with a full head of "romantic grey" hair (as Julie had heard the Japanese call it). They had one son, Tony, now in his midthirties, and a daughter, Mary Francis, a little younger, about Julie's age.

For most of his life in New Jersey, Frankie had done well in "private carting," a term for the sanitation business that conveyed a whole bunch of connections to restaurants, construction sites, the local police, and the Brooklyn "families" who took care of their own. Julie understood the connection from a personal experience, trying to get the cops to do something about a private carter that had garbage trucks grinding away under the windows of her Greenwich Village brownstone all hours of the night. When she asked the cop who arrived from the local precinct in response to her call what he could do about the noise, he stared at her with a serious expression and said, "Lady, that there is private carting."

"So?" Julie had countered, "What can I do about them?"

With a perfectly straight face, the cop advised her, "You could move to a quiet street in Staten Island." Julie got it.

As Frankie grew older, private carting proved too much for his back, so he "retired" to bartending in a local establishment. When the weather and the long bar hours prevented even that limited employment, Arlene and Frankie had moved to Florida's Gold Coast, where their son fell into a tub of butter by marrying the daughter of a wealthy car dealer who put him in the business. Their daughter, a smart, decent person whom Julie really liked, became a social worker. Arlene became a super saleswoman in a Bloomies in an upscale mall where her commissions substantially augmented her low wages, while Frankie's occasional stints of undemanding work brought in additional income. It was Arlene and Frankie who'd urged Lottie and Sol to move to North Miami, a relatively easy drive away, and even after Sol's death, they had remained close to Julie's aunt. They were very good to her; Lottie was the first one to say it. Arlene brought her discount items from Bloomies, and Tony, who had moved on from his lucrative but boring car dealership to the management of a classy Palm Beach restaurant, always loaded up their car trunk with hampers of food that not only saved Lottie hours of cooking but also were a useful chip in the rituals of favor giving and reciprocity that characterized the complex interactions of retirees' social life.

Yet, Lottie had sometimes confessed to Julie that there was a certain tension there. Now she spoke to Julie in thoughtful, measured tones about her concerns. "You see, Julie, Frankie's not really working any more. And even with her commissions, how much can Arlene make at Bloomies? Me? I think she'd work just to get out of the house no matter how low the pay was, and of course, she's an excellent saleswoman, looks beautiful in the clothes; am I right?"

"Yes," Julie sincerely agreed, "a real fashionista."

"Okay then," Lottie went on. "Tony, to be fair, did terrific on his own merit. From hanging around his father, he got to love the restaurant business. And he's got talent, no question. His restaurant sent him to Rome to some special culinary school to learn a new kind of Italian cooking; they call it nouvelle Italian—I think that's the right pronunciation. Just as tasty but not so fattening, like whole wheat pasta and olive oil instead of butter on the garlic bread. That's what they put in the hampers they brought down; we can try it out. Now Tony, he came down with Arlene and Frankie, he has the idea to open up his own restaurant. The problem is, that requires a small fortune. The competition is fierce. Okay, the help is cheap, not the chefs, but the waiters, maybe, busboys, plenty of illegals who take any job they can get. Tony says he's got lots of investors already; it's sure to be a success, like this trendy new restaurant called Mickey's in that fancy Ritz Carlton Hotel up toward North Beach." Aunt Lottie paused thoughtfully for a moment and then said, "Maybe we could try a lunch there, Julie, to see how such a place looks, if it's got a lot of customers. The new idea is Mediterranean, fresh fish—I don't know, Julie, doesn't that spoil awfully fast? It's not like selling sweaters where you can put the leftovers on sale at the end of the season. So the long and the short of it is that they wanted to know if I had a few dollars I wanted to invest in this new place."

Julie was lost for words. "You know, Aunt Lottie, my family isn't really up on financial investments. My mom and I have our teaching pension money in the most conservative investments; everyone sort of laughed at us because we only bought the safest tax free bonds with our leftover savings, and they were getting such low interest rates. When Daddy died suddenly like he did, he had a life insurance policy that left Mom a decent amount, and of course, she gets part of his foundation pension, too, but we don't take risks with money is what I mean. And now with the stock market crashing and all, I think maybe we did the right thing. A lot of older people who thought they had good retirements coming now have to go back to work."

"Yes, Julie," Aunt Lottie agreed. "So here's the question: Is this a good time for me to invest in an upscale restaurant?" *Maybe you should ask Dr. Galbinki,* Julie felt like saying. *He's the kind of guy Tony probably hopes to attract to his fresh shrimp with popcorn and pricey wine cellar.* "On the up-side," Julie responded, "Frankie and Tony know the business; they must have cased out the potential. All those Russian 'biznessmen' grabbing up the new condos on the Beach probably line up at the 'in' places with their trophy girlfriends. We could try a lunch at this Mickey's when the doctor gives you the okay, and check out the lay of the land," Julie offered. "But I don't feel qualified to give you financial advice."

"That's fine. I know what I know. Which is to say, even if Tony's new restaurant is a big success, I'm an old lady; do I need this aggravation? Arlene and Frankie, their money situation hasn't been so great the past few years. That's why they're asking me. True, they've been good to me. But in the past few years I've also helped out with a few things they needed and really couldn't afford themselves. I bought them their new freezer and washer-dryer. I didn't mind. And, of course, I gave them $5,000 for Mary Francis's wedding, like I promised, just like for your sister's, and for yours, too, when that happens. But their new swimming pool was supposed to be a *loan*, and they still haven't paid me back for it. Maybe they think I have more money than I really do. Or they think I'm leaving them money in my will, but they figure they'd rather have it now when they need it rather than later. They don't know I don't have a will. Just our joint bank accounts, Julie; your name is on everything. And my burial is prepaid; your mom has the papers, and I'm leaving all my jewelry to you. I'm not going to sell it; it wouldn't bring more than a couple of thousand dollars anyway. Who knows if I'll live long enough to see any payback from an investment? I haven't got that much time left, do I?"

Julie pooh-poohed her aunt's remark about her age but saw her comments as a good opening for the idea that maybe it was time for Lottie to consider moving out of her present residence to a better kind of retirement community. A safer, more upscale environment, maybe an assisted living with a pleasant dining room, some structured activities, and medical facilities on the premises so she wouldn't have to worry about midnight emergency room visits when she felt unwell. Surprisingly, her aunt's eyes lit up when Julie tentatively broached her notion. "Maybe Mom would even come down for a week to look around with us, and Charlotte could drive us in her big car so you'd be comfortable," Julie suggested.

"Yes, now is the time to do it, when the weather's not so hot," Aunt Lottie agreed. "Let's see what Dr. Galbinki says when he comes in tonight."

They didn't have long to wait until the doctor appeared, greeting Aunt Lottie effusively. "How's my favorite patient?" he asked, and without waiting for a reply, he conducted a brief examination, after closing the curtain and asking Julie to leave for a few minutes. After the brief examination, he opened the curtain and Julie reentered the room. He said that, having seen Lottie's computer charts, he'd given the directions for her to leave the next afternoon. "I'll want to see you in about a week at my office," he told Julie's aunt and then turned to Julie, as if she were a secretary, and reminded her to make an appointment with his receptionist. Before he could exit, Aunt Lottie told him brightly of their idea of moving her to a new apartment, maybe in a better area. "Somewhere not too far from your office, of course."

To Julie's surprise, Dr. Galbinki was very enthusiastic about the suggestion. "Yes, I think it may be time, Lottie," he said. "It doesn't have to be near my office; that's quite an expensive area. There's an excellent assisted-living facility—we call them ALFs for short," he explained to Julie—"that I'm affiliated with; they have a medical unit where I see many of their residents, and I'm sure you'll find it just what you're looking for." He took a card from his wallet and handed it to Lottie. *Boy, that was quick*, Julie noted, *what, does he get a commission for steering his adoring patients to this place?* Aunt Lottie thanked him profusely, and even Julie figured it couldn't hurt to include that particular ALF on their "pilgrimage" as she was beginning to think of it. Now that Lottie was so excited about the upcoming possibility of a move, she forgot to ask Dr. Galbinki what had happened to Mrs. Greene in the other bed. But when she herself was discharged the next day, she did ask Clarice again what had happened to Mrs. Greene.

"Don't fret yourself, Mrs. Freund," said the aide kindly. "She's gone to a better place. We all have to go sometime, and compared to many people, a person who dies of old age is quite lucky. She seems to have passed peacefully in her sleep. Isn't that as much as any of us can hope for?"

Chapter Six

A week later, Aunt Lottie got a clean bill of health from Dr. Galbinki. When Julie called her mom to tell her about their plans to look for a new place for her aunt, her mother agreed to fly down and help in the search. She arrived in a taxi at Lottie's apartment as Julie and Charlotte were organizing a load of articles and brochures about various facilities for older people.

"What about a move to an apartment in a better neighborhood, with a night caregiver added to Charlotte's daytime hours?" Julie offered as the first suggestion.

Her aunt immediately scotched the night caregiver suggestion. "I don't want anyone else sleeping in my house," she asserted. "It's one thing when you or Jean"—she nodded toward Julie's mom—"come down, but I had a husband, that was enough sharing a bedroom and bathroom for me. I like eating my early breakfast and watching the TV news by myself, and spending the time before Charlotte comes taking my bath and putting on my outfits and my makeup alone; I don't need help. Charlotte knows my ways, and I hope she can still come over a couple of days a week, drive me to shopping and the doctors, take walks with me—I know I need help in that area, my feet are so bad, but no 'roommates' 24-7."

"And remember, Julie," Charlotte pointed out, "Lottie doesn't drive, and any decent residential neighborhood she could afford would typically have lousy or no public transportation. Those nice residential areas have hardly any shops within walking distance, so even if Lottie walked with me, there'd be nothing to interest us. If Lottie enjoyed gardening and taking care of a small private house, those are the best deals right now because of the foreclosure disaster that has hit South Florida hard, but I don't think that's for her." Lottie nodded her emphatic agreement. "What's the sense of moving to a neighborhood not too much different than this one, just a different set of dangerous roads to cross, another high school on the block, another bunch of noisy kids living next door. No sense at all."

"Years ago," Julie's mom pointed out, "co-ops or even rentals in South Miami Beach would have been a good choice, but now the Beach is gentrified out of sight, all glass skyscrapers with gunslinging guards to protect the prosperous young professionals, two-income couples, and the few really wealthy seniors who can afford to live there."

"Okay, let's move on," they all agreed. Julie suggested one of the gated communities that had proliferated over the last thirty years along the Gold Coast. There'd be people Lottie's age, some structured activities, sort of like a cruise ship, that would introduce her to new friends, and probably lots of women sharp enough to get up the killer canasta games she was used to. "Great idea," Julie's mom said. "How about that Century 21 or whatever it's called? I stayed at the one in West Palm Beach for a week once, and it was actually a lot of fun. *Two* rooms of pool tables, an aerobics class every morning; there were actually sidewalks outside the place where you could walk to a mall with a library and a Starbucks. Free buses took you shopping, and for three bucks one of the inmates—a joke, a joke," she hastened to say, "—would even drive you to the nearby clubs at night and pick you up."

Julie knew her mother would never retire to that kind of community; she'd often said that the only way she'd leave New York City was in a pine box, and if they found her dead in a snowdrift one winter, so be it. But at least she wasn't voicing that particularly unhelpful sentiment now, and Julie silently applauded her effort to enter the spirit of the discussion.

Lottie dismissed her sister's suggestion with a "feh" and a wave. "First of all, Jean, it's West Palm Beach Century *Village*, not Century 21; that's the

New York department store all the tourists go to; they give you a wheelbarrow to carry around the stuff you want to buy. West Palm was the first Century Village built, so it's quite run down. The people who came there years ago were the 'young old'; now they're the 'old old,' and with tons of grandchildren coming down, it's like a summer camp. I know, my friends told me about it. Anyway, it's too far from my doctors, and all these gated communities have nothing to see if you do take a walk except bushes. Again, *feh!*"

"Okay, let's study the map and circle the areas that are close in and still affordable, and maybe there are different kinds of assisted-living places, those ALFs, that would be a good compromise," Julie suggested. "That way you could be independent, Aunt Lottie, have your own little apartment, but still have some activities you'd enjoy with people like yourself. I have lots of brochures about them; they're the newest form of retirement community. Of course, they vary tremendously. Some are just sort of like apartment hotels with a small reception and security staff and visiting medical people, but others seem to be much more upscale. Don't forget, Dr. Galbinki gave us that card; we certainly have to include a visit there."

"Good idea," chimed in Charlotte, "there's another place, near here, we might visit. It's worth a look even if just for the future. It's halfway between an informal ALF and a nursing home, but they have to call it a nursing home in order to qualify for state and federal assistance through Medicaid. But it's a mom-and-pop operation; the owners are decent people, not like these hedge-fund investors who are taking over a lot of these facilities and turning them into cash cows. All they care about is the bottom line without giving a darn how their patients are treated. This couple lives on the premises themselves. They have good continuity of medical staff, and they check their practical nurses' and aides' licenses and credentials pretty thoroughly, which a lot of these places don't."

As soon as she heard the words "nursing home," though, Aunt Lottie protested. "No, no, no nursing homes. Haven't you read about that killer nurse—it turned out she didn't even have a real nurse's license—who was running a scam at some nursing home stuck away in Miami someplace, poor people, mostly, probably without many visitors; that's how they choose them, you see," she added knowledgeably. "She'd get her patients to give her checks for $1,000 in return for the 'extra special care' she promised them, and then after she had their money, she would poison or smother them and get the local doctor to sign their death certificates that they died from 'old age.'"

Charlotte did agree with Lottie that some nursing homes probably deserved their bad rep, even the ones run by different religious groups. She acknowledged that some had even been sued recently for neglect in letting patients die, and in another, some of the hired workers and patients had turned out to be ex-convicts for things like sexual assault. "Let's face it," Charlotte added, "what kind of staff can you expect with the wages they pay? They look at the patients as people 'who are going to die soon anyway,' so they do the nasty jobs like hand feeding or changing diapers without respect for their dignity. The advantage is that the government pays a large part of the patients' costs and is *supposed*"—Charlotte drawled the word sarcastically—"to provide oversight. Patients can't be kicked out on the street for not paying their maintenance the way they can in some of the better-class ALFs, where assessments and cost upgrades that weren't in the contract can pile up after a person buys in."

"Charlotte knows what she's talking about," Julie and her mom agreed, but by consensus her nursing home suggestion went to the bottom of the list.

The following day, with Charlotte at the wheel of her big, old Buick, the four of them rode around checking out available facilities, interviewing the managers in each facility that looked promising, and picking up yet more brochures. The managers were "much of a muchness" as Jean quipped, paraphrasing from *Alice in Wonderland*. They were basically salespeople mouthing the conventional pieties and sentimental clichés beloved by the retirement facility industry. While their brochures exploded with purple prose about the modern refurbishment and attractive décor, too much of what they saw were rundown complexes similar to Aunt Lottie's current residence: sulky-looking aides were manhandling near-comatose patients; the narrow hallways led to simple rooms that qualified as apartments only through the grace of two-burner hot plates and half-fridges "from the year 1," as Aunt Lottie observed crustily.

Others were attractive, but hardly new, U-shaped apartment houses facing pleasant enough patios and bathtub-sized pools, but though the apartments did provide modest cooking spaces, several of the managers admitted that they did not encourage it. "We don't take the mentally ill or seriously incapacitated," one more honest than the rest confessed, "but we still fear that through carelessness or forgetfulness someone might set their place on fire. We encourage our residents to eat family style in our lovely dining room where we do try to serve nutritious, tasty meals three times a day."

Aunt Lottie took one look at the residents milling around the "clubhouse" and the dining area and frowned. "Only one step above a nursing home," she complained with some justice. "I don't want to eat with these people every day and month and year. It's not the worst we've seen, but I hope I can do better."

They all agreed, shuffled that brochure down the stack, and drove somewhat farther out to a rather desolate gated community with a sleepy-looking guard reading a newspaper who genially waved them in. "No questions, no nothing, we could have been the Christmas underwear bomber," Charlotte noted immediately. Actually, the living quarters were not bad, townhouse-type structures, two or three connected together. A friendly resident invited them in to look at her place. It was nicely furnished, and the woman herself, around Lottie's age, was neatly dressed in the type of matching polyester pantsuit that Lottie herself favored. She told them that many people did cook in their own apartments, but the dining room did in fact serve fairly edible food and was kept very clean. "There's really no place nearby to do food shopping," she admitted, "and not much to do outside the area. In fact, most of the husbands here car pool to a Home Depot about an hour away for part-time work, and pick up takeout on the way home. Or we eat in the dining room with our cliques. It's not a cruise ship, but it suffices." To Lottie's question about the activities, the woman truthfully replied that the clubhouse itself wasn't much to rave about: a few pool tables, card tables, and shuffleboard sets in a corner and a large flat-screen TV with a DVD player that showed pretty decent movies once a week. Aunt Lottie's interest was piqued when the woman said there were some dynamite canasta games; they even had tournaments. But after thanking the woman for her candid remarks, they walked back to the car thinking it just wasn't lively enough for Aunt Lottie. "Okay, it wasn't the no-goes, more like the slow-goes, but definitely not the go-goes," Julie's mom remarked as they got back in the car.

By the end of the fourth day, Julie's mom's enthusiasm was evaporating. She just didn't have the temperament for it: schlepping in and out of the car all day, Aunt Lottie beside Charlotte suspiciously reviewing each brochure, while in the back seat Julie took copious notes and tried to put the best face on any place Aunt Lottie seemed the least bit interested in. In a stage whisper to Julie that Aunt Lottie was meant to hear, Jean sarcastically tore the masks off some of the more oily facility managers they encountered and figuratively ripped their over-the-moon literature to shreds. Aunt Lottie agreed. At this last "war meeting" held around the dining room table, Jean was ready to throw in the towel. "The brochures all lie, and these places are just after your money," she groused, exhausted. But Aunt Lottie was enjoying herself with the upper hand in a buyer's market, as she did at the mall, and was not ready to throw in the towel. "Tomorrow, let's look at Dr. Galbinki's recommendation," she decided, "then, Jean, you can go home."

Chapter Seven

Early the next morning, they set off in Charlotte's "great blue whale" for the ALF Dr. Galbinki had recommended. "Miami Palms, here we come," Julie trilled as she and her mom slid in the back seat. She directed Charlotte along I-95 to the neighborhood of the ALF, according to the directions that Mrs. Murchison, the ALF manager, had given her precisely on the phone this morning when she'd confirmed their appointment. "Now, when you exit the expressway, do lock your doors and close the windows," she had warned Julie. "Our beautiful facility is well protected from the surrounding area, but one always has to be careful. Dr. Galbinki told me you'd be coming," she added. "That's a special recommendation." *Of us or your ALF?* Julie wondered with a sardonic grunt.

As they neared Miami Palms, Julie looked closely out the closed car window at the neighborhood about which Mrs. Murchison had warned her. It was a mix of low-rise housing developments and small single-family bungalows, whose residents she knew were mainly Haitian immigrants. Many of the individual dwellings were brightly painted and had colorful flower boxes in the windows. Some elderly women chattered among themselves as they sat out front on the postage stamp–sized lawns or on the benches of a small project playground, keeping an eye on the young children clambering noisily around the colorful equipment or riding their three-wheelers or

scooters up and down the sidewalks. Julie contemplated the intergenera-
tional mix of children and "grannies"—though they might in fact be "aun-
ties" or other members of an extended family in which three or even four
generations lived together or close by. How different these lively streets were
from the more upscale or even middling-level retirement communities they
had visited on their "pilgrimage," she reflected. Most Americans who retired
to Florida were cut off from seeing their families on an everyday basis, and
visits from their children and grandchildren were strategically planned,
carefully manicured events, often revolving around family activities such as
jaunts to Disney World where the grandparents weren't included.

The contrast with Little Haiti reminded Julie of another of her family
interviews in India. She had encountered a grandmother living with her
son and his family who had asked Julie, with some confusion, "Could it be
true, what I've heard, that in America parents have to make an appointment to see their children or grandchildren. That can't be true, can it?"
she'd asked, the wrinkles furrowing her forehead a she peered intently at
Julie. She'd turned tenderly toward the granddaughter who translated by
her side as Julie had made a real effort to explain the difference between
Indian and American culture and society as it affected families, especially
the care of the elderly. But Julie could see from the grandmother's expression that it was a losing battle. She might understand that many American
wives, like her own daughter-in-law, worked long hours and had long
commutes to and from work. They could not give up their jobs—sometimes very high-paying jobs that were essential to the family's income for
luxuries, or even necessities—in order to provide caregiving to an aged
parent. But that American teenagers had their own schedules jammed with
social, athletic, and other activities that prevented their spending time with
their grandparents appeared to elude her. As the grandmother sat silent,
waiting, perhaps out of politeness, for Julie to say something more to help
her understand, Julie had turned in consternation to the granddaughter.

"Can you help me out here? I want to explain to your grandma how
in America we have adult day centers that take senior citizens back and
forth to their own homes, where many of them actually prefer to live on

their own, and not share their homes with their children or have teenagers around all the time. Many senior citizens who can afford it actually choose to move away from their families to retirement communities where children are not even allowed."

The granddaughter thought for a moment, then translated slowly so her grandmother could understand these difficult concepts; her grandmother replied in a few words, and the girl sadly told Julie, "I'm sorry, she says she can't understand."

The streets of the typical American retirement village were generally quiet and empty, and even in ordinary South Florida residential areas, where some of Julie's own friends, mostly professors at the local colleges, lived, people walking on the streets were a rarity. Once, when staying at a friend's house in South Florida, she had decided to stroll the mile or so to the nearest library; a police car pulled up, and the officer stuck his head out to ask if she needed assistance. When she explained that she was just walking to the local library, the officer had looked at her strangely and admonished, "Well, be careful, nobody walks in Florida."

Out of the car window, now, Julie also noticed, however, the more troublesome signs of the lively streets they were passing through: knots of young men in pastel pleated pants, gorgeously colored silk shirts hanging out, and soft leather street shoes, hanging out with their cell phones clamped to their ears or engaging in desultory conversation. Miami had a horrendous unemployment rate, Julie knew, and many of these men were probably without living-wage jobs if they were out here on a weekday morning. Such communities often housed a plague of drug dealers, as she read in the newspapers, and it was usually the innocent ones among the majority of decent working people who became the victims of the drug-related robberies and drive-by shootings. So, however picturesque the scene outside the car windows appeared, Julie checked that the doors were securely locked. Then she argued with herself until they reached the ALF about whether her reaction was racialist, realist, or both. *How complicated even this microcosm of the world is,* she sighed. *But that's what makes being a cultural anthropologist so interesting.*

As Charlotte passed the Second Avenue Haitian market and small unpretentious Caribbean groceries and clothing shops that lined the commercial streets, Julie bit her lower lip in concern about whether Aunt Lottie would feel fearful about living in an ALF surrounded by such a neighborhood. But her aunt's expression didn't change as she looked out the window.

It had been agreed that whichever facility Aunt Lottie chose in the end, she would still have Charlotte in for several days a week at least, to drive her to the supermarket, do some advance cooking for her, take her on excursions or to her Hadassah meetings, and of course, drive her to her doctors' appointments. Julie had insisted on that last one since her aunt's first heart surgery. She knew that Lottie was of the old school to whom physicians were "saints" whose diagnoses or treatments could never be questioned, and she relied on Charlotte to take detailed notes at each visit so that Julie or her mom would be kept up to date in their frequent phone calls.

As Mrs. Murchison had claimed, the Miami Palms facility itself was really quite beautiful. As they pulled up to the entrance, they saw ahead of them a complex of lovely, Spanish-style buildings set in a lush garden of bright pink bougainvillea, carmine flame trees, coconut palms, and even a few towering royal palms. A tiled Spanish fountain played in the middle of glowing green lawn. The tall, decorative wrought-iron fence that surrounded the facility was interrupted by an ornate gate that stood open to a cubicle; this was manned by a smartly uniformed and armed young black guard who carefully scrutinized Charlotte's and Julie's photo IDs. Julie wondered if he was a local man, perhaps an Iraq war vet. In work-starved Miami, this employment was probably much appreciated and might lead to a future security firm or even law enforcement position. Julie realized that, while the ALF seemed like a world apart from its surrounding neighborhood, it might actually serve as a welcome source of employment for the young adults and even older people who lived nearby.

The guard telephoned Mrs. Murchison, who said she would meet them at the small parking lot near the gatehouse. In a matter of minutes, a shocking-pink golf cart drew up. In the driver's seat was a bouffant-coiffed deeply tanned matron of indeterminate age who wore a pink pantsuit and a white mesh broad-brimmed hat. Riding shotgun next to her was a tall, white poodle, elaborately clipped like a topiary bush, sitting upright with its front paws leaning on the dashboard ledge. Julie thought she'd been dropped down the rabbit hole but gamely recovered as Mrs. Murchison introduced herself.

"Three can squeeze comfortably in the back, ladies," she told them, but Julie's mother replied with alacrity that she'd be happy to walk rather than ride. "If you're sure," Mrs. Murchison said doubtfully. "Okay, we'll meet you back at the admin building in about half an hour." Mrs. Murchison pointed to the historic brownstone, brick-and-tiled edifice that served as the ALF offices. *The whole place isn't more than a few city blocks big,* Julie's mother fumed inwardly; *we could all walk. I should point to my feet and inform her that these are feet, f-e-e-t, an archaic word unknown in Florida for the last sixty years, but still in the dictionary. They're not round, like wheels, but they carry some of us along pretty well if we practice a lot.* As Jean strode away, the "troika" was whirled off on the tour of the "campus."

As she drove, Mrs. Murchison emphasized the positive aspects of the facility in the cheery tone of a kindergarten teacher. Julie felt at once that the architecture was a plus point. Although the residence "pods," as their bizarre guide named them, might not have been authentic Art Deco structures from the thirties or forties, they approximated the now-desirable homes and hotels of that fashionable era in their rounded fronts, cream-colored stucco skins with orange and green trim, and slanted roofs that extended over pleasant porches. Julie favored them far more than the luxurious glass towers that had replaced their originals up and down Miami Beach as far north as Sunny Isles. As Mrs. Murchison drove the cart past the swimming pool, Julie noted that it was large enough to permit real lap swimming, unlike most retirement village pools that barely let you take three strokes before you banged your head on the end, not that Aunt Lottie had any intention of using it, as she made clear.

On the golf cart's final lap, Julie noticed a group of elderly women with a few men strewn among them, all dressed in decent-looking clothes but with something askew about their appearance. Some shirts were not fully tucked in, some shorts bagged ludicrously as if they were not sized for the person who wore them, and a few folks wore faded baseball caps at odd angles or other unattractive headgear. They presented a depressing picture, and Julie broke into Mrs. Murchison's cheery script to point toward the doorway where they milled around. "And who are those folks?" she asked brightly. Mrs. Murchison rapidly swerved the cart in the opposite direction and answered dismissively over her shoulder.

"Oh, those are our nursing home clientele waiting for the van to their dining room. They use different facilities than our ALF clients."

With the tour over, Mrs. Murchison deposited Charlotte, Lottie, and Julie at the door of the admin building. "Please go in; I'll be right there," she told them. Julie's mom was already seated in one of the elegant rattan, chintz-pillowed chairs that were scattered across the light and airy lobby.

"It was an informative tour," Julie told her mom as Lottie and Charlotte took seats nearby. "She's just coming back to tell us about the dining facilities and the rooms themselves, which is how the costs are figured. She'll show us a couple of different options, okay?"

"Is the poodle coming, too?" Julie's mom asked with a snarky grin. "Maybe he's an honorary human? Or maybe he's like a bloodhound. He sniffs us all and then leads us to the room he thinks we can afford."

"Jean!" Aunt Lottie warned her sister. "I like this place. For me, this is serious business. Maybe they don't take everyone who applies. I'm sure Dr. Galbinki doesn't recommend all his patients here. Maybe to someone like ritzy Mrs. Greene in the next bed he would give a card. Not that every person isn't as good as every other person. But the people here look more my type than in most of those place we visited." Julie, Charlotte, and even Jean looked thoughtfully around the lobby. What Lottie said was so. The casual dress of the other women in the lobby was fashionable enough for their age but not inappropriately youthful; their hairdos were mostly carefully dyed or white bouffant styles such as Lottie herself wore; and their footwear, which Julie regarded as an important economic and social indicator, was shined and not run down at the heels. Julie agreed with Lottie; they did not look like the kind of women who would walk around the campus in housedresses or "those hideous gym 'gotkas,'" as Lottie described them. "Bad enough on the young, but on older women, *feh!*"

Mrs. Murchison returned and gathered Aunt Lottie's companions together. "You know a few apartments in some of the pods have small kitchenettes for those who like taking their meals alone"—she furrowed her forehead as if to imply that only the insane would do such a thing, and Julie momentarily recalled that the ancient Greeks had a similar view. "But most of our clients prefer the tasty, nutritious meals we serve in our really lovely dining room." She led them across the lobby as she talked, and yes, it was true again: the dining room was most attractive, with large windows whose thin white curtains fluttered in the light breeze, and tablecloths of a pretty flowered design graced the tables for eight. As they walked back to the lobby, Mrs. Murchison said she would thank Dr. Galbinki for recommending Miami Palms to them and congratulated Lottie on having such a fine physician. "The excellent Dr. Galbinki is one of the 'on call' doctors for our infirmary and nursing home adjunct facility," she said self-importantly. "And now I want to offer you some of the brochures that describe our facilities and take you up to some typical apartments that happen to be empty at the moment."

Here's where the rubber hits the road, Julie reminded herself. *Of course management creates a caring, harmonious atmosphere, but bottom line, these facilities were real estate investments, and if they didn't show a profit they were out of business. Yet, Aunt Lottie seemed genuinely pleased with Miami Palms, and if it cost a bit more, well, with Bobby gone, what else did she have to spend her money on? It was a better investment than Tony's restaurant. Let her go through it all, and then they'd worry about it. She'd heard that a lot of these places would make a deal for the social security . . . and Aunt Lottie's was at the top, having worked at a good salary for so many years.*

That afternoon, Julie, her mom, Aunt Lottie, and Charlotte held their last "war meeting." Julie spread out the Miami Palms brochures. The apartments they'd seen had been cozy enough, if not as roomy as Lottie's present one, and she wouldn't need to buy new furniture, just take the best of what she already owned. The sliding scale of fees would depend on which apartment Lottie took. Lottie said she wanted one of the apartments with the tiny kitchenette, even if it was a bit pricier.

"I'd like to be able to have a cup of tea in private with Charlotte or Julie, or if I make a special friend, not sit in the lounge and have everyone hear my business," she asserted. "And you know, I always hated living on the ground floor here, anyone could look in my windows . . . and it's always dark, easy for a robber to climb in. I'd like to be on a higher floor with lots of light."

"I never knew you felt that way," Jean told her older sister. "Of course, robberies could come from the inside, too, even in a place like this. So, for security, the floor may not matter. But as to the rest, I see your point. And listen, Lottie," she continued as she uncharacteristically covered her sister's hand with her own, "you got a nice life insurance settlement from Sol; you have your pension, and all your life you worked hard and took a lot of knocks from Papa that I was spared because I was 'the baby.' Maybe this place is a little more luxurious than you planned on, but don't let a few dollars stand in your way. You know I have some savings to put toward the extras, too. Treat yourself a little."

Julie supported her mom's opinion with reference to the Miami Palms brochure. "Look, they have outings to the convention center, and with Charlotte still on board, you'll be able to walk around the neighborhood, window-shop, and see people on the street, not only old people. Now let's do the money," she wisecracked.

"That's for you and Lottie to discuss tomorrow," Jean said. "My plane leaves at noon; you can just keep me in the loop by phone." She walked Charlotte out to her car and thanked her for helping out.

"I think this may be just the right place for Mrs. Freund," Charlotte told her. "I gather you and your sister are something like chalk and cheese, but I know she appreciated your coming down."

"You're right about that," Jean replied. "My Julie is better with her than I am. She has the anthropologist's ability to inhabit different points of view; she's patient, nonjudgmental, and able to move at the slower pace down here. They have almost a whole month to settle this thing. I think it will go well."

❧ Chapter Eight

When Julie's mom had left, Julie and her aunt laid out their plans. They gathered up Lottie's financial papers from the bedroom dresser drawer where Lottie also kept her little treasure trove of jewelry for Julie to inherit "when the time came," as she said. Slyly, Lottie picked up her diamond heart looped through a thick gold chain and hung it around Julie's neck, as she did every time Julie came down to visit. "We haven't had time to talk about it yet, but you mentioned something about a serious fella, right? You'll wear this at your wedding, and I'll have the picture right here on my bureau with Sol and Bobby's."

Then Lottie frowned and muttered something about how it looked like her things had been moved around. "But who could it be?" she wondered softly to herself. Julie pooh-poohed her concern but then recalled Arlene and Frankie's visit to her aunt's house to deposit the food they'd brought down. Could they have checked her dresser drawers just to see if they could find some indications of her financial situation or even a will? *Well, we certainly have no proof of that,* Julie admonished herself. *Anyway, even if they found some papers, there's not much they could do about them.*

Julie admired the way her aunt had proudly managed on her own since her widowhood, and even before that if truth be told. She knew more about money management than Sol, and though her circumstances hadn't allowed her to go to college, she knew business and accounting better than a lot of professors with degrees. It'd been a tough decision, picking herself up with Sol and making the move into a new place, a new culture really. For there was a definite culture of aging in Florida. And all the different kinds of retirement facilities functioned as subcultures, processing the values and norms of American society in their own ways. A common theme of the "old old" in South Florida was basking in the reflected glory of their children's and grandchildren's accomplishments. Julie was Lottie's chip in the unspoken competition between her and her neighbors' sons who were successful professionals or businessmen, and Julie played her role appropriately. Her aunt would introduce her to a neighbor as "my niece Julie, a big anthropologist in New York; she's just finished an important book on India," and Julie would nod demurely, but not too humbly. By modeling her visits on her ethnographic fieldwork, working as a participant-observer and inserting herself into a different culture, Julie was able to truly enjoy her visits with her aunt.

For many years, she and her mom had traded off weeks in Florida with Aunt Lottie, but Julie was by far the better guest. What did Julie care if her aunt packed her closet shelves full of Cheerios bought on sale "for a rainy day" or kept plastic slipcovers on her couch? Julie didn't mock the malls as "God's waiting room" or laugh at their storefront medical offices with the first names of the presiding physician emblazoned over the doorway. Did Steve's Pain Clinic or Harvey's Wellness Center, All Welcome, indicate that less well-off or less medically savvy patients could get some relief from pain or illness in such places? Actually, Julie reconsidered, she didn't really know anything about these places. They were simply cultural spaces that she hadn't assessed yet.

Unlike her mom, when Julie took her aunt out for an early bird dinner, she didn't grimace in embarrassment when the waiters at Lottie's favorite restaurants would immediately bring over the bread basket with the little bag for the "extras": the leftover rolls that Lottie liked to take home. Aunt Lottie ignored her younger sister's exasperation at the hoarding. "I'm just an old lady; what do they care?" she'd laugh with the waiters, and they'd laugh with her. She was a generous tipper, so they couldn't care less.

But Julie's biggest advantage to Aunt Lottie was that she drove without complaint. While Julie shared her mother's views about the American addiction to cars, excessive speed, and driving while talking on a cell phone or texting, she kept her opinions in check on her Florida visits. Aunt Lottie regaled her with stories of Julie's mother's driving style, cursing the young people who slid in and out of the lanes like demons in their sports cars or those huge SUV things that looked like armored cars. "Once she shouted out the window at some man in one of those huge square metal Hummer cars that if he needed a vehicle like that, he should be fighting in Afghanistan," she told Julie. "I was afraid some day one of these people she yelled at would drive us off the road. You know how to relax a little in the car. It's more pleasant to go somewhere, am I right?"

Julie worked all afternoon and for the next several days with her aunt, figuring out the financials, talking to some of the people at the bank where Lottie had most of her money. Finally, the time had come for Lottie to say yes or no. "It's yes, Julie," Lottie made the decision. "I'd like to keep my apartment for a couple of months until I see how the ALF works out. Then, when you come down again, we can settle up everything permanently."

"Excellent idea," Julie replied. "I'll make an appointment with Mrs. Murchison to get all the necessary papers and confirm a moving date and so on. I'd like to have a lawyer look at all the forms and answer every question. Then we can arrange the move, speak to your landlady here, and make piles of stuff for the giveaways and the things that will stay. It won't take so long. We'll have plenty of time to enjoy ourselves, eat out, and go to the Art Deco weekend on the Beach. I can easily come down again anyway after my spring semester's finished. I thought of asking Mike to take a week or two down here with me; we'd stay at a hotel, of course, but I could take him to your new ALF and you could meet him. He could help us with the final move, too." Her aunt was so pleased at the idea that Julie felt tears spill into her eyes. They hadn't really had a chance to talk about Mike yet, but there was still plenty of time. Julie would show Lottie the photo of Mike and her looking almost dementedly happy on a Hudson River hike they'd taken in the glowing fall colors, and her aunt could ask about the relationship to her heart's content. "That will be perfect," Lottie said. "Now we have a lot to do."

The first thing was to advise Gert, the landlady, who lived in the complex, which she also owned, that Lottie *might* be moving out permanently by the summer but still wanted to retain her apartment until then. Julie was surprised that Gert seemed unhappy with that arrangement. *What is she losing?* Julie asked herself. But as Gert talked about her future plans for the complex, perhaps renovating it and turning it into a nursing home or some other kind of retirement facility for which she might get government assistance, Julie understood that she wanted the current tenants out as fast as possible. The newer immigrant tenants weren't such a problem. Most of them probably didn't have leases anyway, and, who knows, half of them might be undocumented immigrants with no recourse but to keep under the radar and not bring the ICE (Immigration and Customs Enforcement) down on their heads. But the seniors were a different story. Laws protected them, and you couldn't just shove them out the door. Gert was not a bad person really, just a little greedy, and she had, after all, known Lottie for many, many years. "If I do move permanently to my new place, Gert," Lottie told her, "anything that I don't take with me, that Julie doesn't want, you can have. I don't really have more than a couple of friends here now, only Lou and Lillian really, and they don't need any stuff, for sure." The landlady thanked her, and seeing it was a done deal, wished Lottie well on her new move. "You're very brave," she said, and Lottie replied, surprisingly, "Yes, I think I am."

"Only Lillian left to tell, Julie," her aunt said. "Since Lou's still in Las Vegas, we'll just wait 'til he comes home to tell him. Oh, will he be surprised. I bet he won't be too happy about it either. But he drives, so if he wants to see me, that's no problem. Miami Palms is only a short distance from South Beach with all its nice little restaurants; he can just take me out to lunch some time," she asserted with satisfaction.

Lillian Goodman had been Lottie's next-door neighbor since the early days, another of the original tenants. Julie had met her many times and always enjoyed talking with her. Lillian was a novelty among Aunt Lottie's friends; in fact, Julie had never met anyone like her. Lillian had grown up in a small midwestern town; her father had owned a dry goods store, in which Lillian worked part-time during high school. During World War II, a wave of patriotism rushed over the United States, and like many of her male counterparts, Lillian wanted to enlist in the service. But she didn't want to be a WAC (Women's Army Corps) or a WAVE (Women Accepted for Volunteer Emergency Service); she was determined to fly a plane. She'd taken flying lessons and gotten a license, but the men's air corps wasn't admitting women pilots yet. Not like Russia, or even Germany, where women were flying combat missions. Even England was using women to ferry planes around England to get them where they needed to be for combat use. It was dangerous duty there, with the antiaircraft batteries and artillery, but the women did a great job and won the respect of their countrymen. Some American women were so eager to join in the war that they'd signed up for the English service.

In the United States, with the support of a few determined women, and the help of First Lady Eleanor Roosevelt, some women's military units were established, but the women weren't flying yet. They did become control tower operators, even though a lot of men opposed this, saying women could not handle the multitasking needed for such work.

"I was outraged," Lillian had told Julie. "Imagine the thinking back then, that women couldn't do any job as good as men. We really proved ourselves. They had a flight training school in Sweetwater, Texas, we were called civilians, couldn't get military standing, but we were trained just like in 'the army way,' living military style, with uniforms, drills, regulations, and even morning reveille. The WASP, or Women Airforce Service Pilots, finally formed up in 1943, and we did amazing things. We flew every plane in the air force to where it was needed, and when the male pilots were afraid to fly the new B-29 Superfortress because of mechanical difficulties experienced during testing, two of our gals took one on a tour of the air bases to show the men how safe the plane was. We did everything: we towed targets for aerial gunnery practice, ran flight checks for recently repaired aircraft, and even served as flight instructors and test pilots, too. We really showed the men. By the end of 1944, when the war was nearly over, a lot of the male pilots who didn't want to be sent to the Pacific succeeded in taking our jobs, and by the end of the year we were deactivated. But even with all our success—and even though over thirty of us died on duty—they still wouldn't give us military status, so no veteran's benefits either, and most of us went back to being housewives and mothers.

"Like a lot of the girls, I got married after I left the service, and who ever heard of us? No one. My husband had served in the war, too; he was a lot older than me but a good man. Of course, our civilian life wasn't as exciting as being a WASP, but all good things come to an end, and I just decided to move on. Some of the girls kept on fighting, though, and in 1977, that conservative senator who ran for president, Barry Goldwater, won us our military status. Now we get veteran's benefits and can be buried in Arlington Cemetery. I'm so proud of that, to be buried with all the other heroes of America's wars. We girls used to get together for reunions; there was a big gathering a couple of years ago to see a film about women pilots, but I couldn't go, stuck in this bed here. But I read all about it. I still got some good friends from those days, we keep in touch."

As soon as Julie and Lottie walked in the apartment, Lillian's two yapping Chihuahuas danced around their legs. Julie knew this pair wasn't the original; Lillian had replaced her beloved pets several times over the years, but she gave them all the same names—Ike and Billy—for General Dwight Eisenhower and General William "Billy" Mitchell—only adding number 2, 3, or whatever. Since Lillian had been practically bedridden for the last several years, she made various arrangements with local teenagers for the dogs' care. Sometimes, Julie would take them out for long walks around the desolate mall or empty streets, as much to get the exercise for herself as for them. One thing Lillian did have, though, was good military medical care through the local VA hospital. They even provided the transportation. Julie never heard her complain—she actually didn't know exactly what caused Lillian's chronic and sometimes acutely painful back problems—and when she visited she always picked up some of the fancy pastries she knew Lillian liked. Lillian was the first one to admit she'd never been an apple pie–baking mom and wasn't about to start now, but she did love every kind of baked goods. Julie and Lottie also brought in their own teabags or instant coffee since they didn't want their visits to be a burden where Lillian felt she had to apologize for not getting up.

"I'll do everything in here, Lillian; you just talk with my aunt," Julie called out from the kitchen. "She has something important to tell you." Lottie seated herself in the comfortable armchair near Lillian's bed and waited for Julie to return with the tea and pastries, placing some of the latter on the hospital-like tray arrangement Lillian glided over her bed.

"Ta da, Lillian," Lottie announced with a flourish. "Guess what? I'm moving. We drove around to a million different places last week, and I found one I think I'll really like. I want to tell you all about it, but the first thing I want to say is, I will miss you terribly. You're probably the only one I'll miss, and I know you can't get out to see me, but whenever Julie visits, we'll come to see you together. And we can talk on the phone as much as we like," Lottie added.

"Oh, Lottie," Lillian said sadly, "I'm so happy for you, but I'll miss you, too. But I'll get news of you alright, through Dr. Galbinki, so you better be a good girl! Since you introduced him to me when he came to your house that time, he's called and even come over a few times to check up on me. And he really is one of the good guys; I never see charges to my Medicare records for those visits. I know they have these pain clinics all over now, but it's so hard for me to get out . . . sometimes he'll just bring me a bottle of pills or give me a shot if I'm really suffering, so I don't have to go down to the VA hospital. Why, that introduction was almost as important to me as the blind date where I met my husband." Lillian winked at Julie. "Who knew that doctors made house visits any more, eh? Before your time, Julie," she chuckled affectionately.

As Lottie and Julie got up to go, Julie advised Lillian that she'd be around for a couple of more weeks and to be sure to call if she needed any special shopping or whatever. "And I will take Ike and Billy out for a couple of more walks," Julie added. "I'll say goodbye to the old neighborhood."

Julie had contacted an elder lawyer recommended by one of her Floridian colleagues, who had looked over the ALF contract carefully with her and proclaimed it "as good as it gets. There're still so many loopholes in the laws that a really fraudulent place or actual criminal types could use them to literally steal from their clients. But that's not quite as common as the newspapers lead you to believe. Your aunt seems to be in good shape financially as regards her obligations with this new ALF. You have my card; if anything comes up later along the way, don't hesitate to call."

And that, Julie thought, *is that.* The moving van came for the furniture Aunt Lottie was taking to the ALF, and Julie helped settle her in her new apartment, which was light and airy and had a small kitchen where they drank endless cups of tea. Charlotte resumed her regular schedule with Lottie, and she and Julie both felt she was fitting in well and were tentatively positive about the move. The weather stayed sunny for the Art Deco weekend, where Julie and her aunt had a fine time in South Beach, strolling the festive streets.

The ALF was much closer to South Beach than Lottie's previous neighborhood, and in very little time, Julie was able to drive to the new Jewish Museum there and the Holocaust Monument just a bit farther up, where she and her aunt pondered the horrible events of the past in Europe. Aunt Lottie and Julie both made a donation, and Lottie had a memorable time afterward talking in Yiddish with the immigrant secretaries in the office. Julie learned something, too, that she hadn't known before. Before World War II, Lottie was the one who'd put together and mailed all the family's care packages to the relatives still stranded in Bialystok, a city that teetered back and forth between Russia and Poland. It was she who had the awful first look at the package marked "No known address; return to sender" in late 1939 when the Germans invaded Poland. And it was she who first intuited that the returned parcel was a message from Europe that the fate of its Jews had now been sealed.

Another day they ate a long late lunch at Mickey's, the upscale restaurant Tony had indicated was the kind of place he wanted to open. They found the atmosphere elegant and the lunch delicious. But no taking home the basket of rolls, Julie had warned her aunt, and no looking at the bill either. *Lottie would have lost her pleasure in the meal if she'd seen it*, Julie knew. They both noted how crowded the place was and figured Tony's idea was a winner.

The remaining days passed quickly, and Julie was already looking forward to her next trip down. In the intervening months, she and her aunt could talk as long as they wanted on Julie's free cell phone weekend minutes, and Julie was sure she'd get the gossip of Lottie's new life in the ALF down to the very last detail.

Chapter Nine

When Julie awoke on the morning of her flight back to New York, she felt satisfied that her trip to Florida had been a grand success. Aunt Lottie seemed in good health, and her move to Miami Palms while retaining her old apartment for a while had worked out well. The new ALF, upscale, but not too expensive, with plenty of services and activities, had an upbeat feel to it. Julie was pleased that her aunt had already signed on with a canasta group of sharp old ladies. "They're older than I am," Lottie had crowed to Julie, "—and ruthless. If somebody can't keep up, they drop them like a hot rock. So far I'm holding my own." Julie thought that, by the time the college semester ended in May, Aunt Lottie would have had enough time to decide if Miami Palms was really what she wanted. Then Julie could come down to help finalize the move from her old apartment. Mike thought he could join her for a couple of weeks, and they could do some hiking and canoeing in the Everglades.

Julie's early afternoon flight to New York left her time for a short visit to her mom's good friend, Howie, who had moved to Sunny Isles, not too far from Aunt Lottie's apartment, where Julie had remained after her aunt moved to the ALF. When Howie had retired from NUNY, he moved to a Florida condo complex of five nondescript buildings now hardly notice-able in the shadow of Trump Towers—*Trump everywhere*, Julie noted in some irritation—and other behemoth luxury high-rises built during the earlier real estate boom along Collins Avenue. Howie buzzed her into his building—*no guards with guns here*, Julie noted, not like some of those luxury condo communities on the Gold Coast. He came down to escort her up to his modest one-bedroom apartment, and Julie commented on the mezuzahs on almost every door. Howie explained that many were left from the original Jewish tenants who had either died or moved to more upscale towns farther north on the Gold Coast. Some of the remaining tenants were Holocaust survivors and, even though very elderly, still lived on their own. Word of mouth had also brought many old lefties to the complex.

"It's wonderful to see you, Julie," Howie said exuberantly. "Thanks for stopping by. So how was your trip?"

"A great place to visit," Julie smiled, "but I could never live here—too many old people."

"Yeah, that's what your mom says," he laughed. "She was surprised when I retired, and even more surprised when I moved down here. She keeps saying, 'I'm never going to retire'; who knows, maybe she won't. And I'd guess for sure she won't move to Florida."

"I was also a little surprised when she told me that you retired, Howie. I know you loved your work."

"I'm a little surprised myself," he agreed. "In America, you are what you do. Retirement raises questions—not only 'what do I do now?' but also 'now that I'm not working, who am I?' It's hard for a lot of retirees to find a meaning in life when they no longer have a job. Their life doesn't seem valuable anymore, to either themselves or the people who know them. One of my colleagues who retired tried to change his mind a month later, but he'd signed the papers and the best he could do was get an adjunct teaching position. 'It came to me when I was filling out my income tax forms,' he once admitted. 'First thing they ask for is occupation, so what was I going to put? It used to be easy: professor of history; now what do I write, bum?'

"And I know the feeling, Julie, believe me," Howie continued. "But there are compensations. Did your mom tell you I bought myself one of those *almost* classic Lincolns? My American Dream came true. Next time you're down, I'll take you for a spin. It's my one bourgeois weakness. I do love that car. It has the high-output GT engine, very hot. It's the Mark VIII 1998 LSC, and the speedometer reads to 140 mph. A gentleman's hotrod, it really moves. Johnny Cash even sang a song about it, *Hot Rod Lincoln*."

"I know it, Howie; it's one of my favorite country-and-western songs. I bet you listen to it all the time," Julie laughingly said. "But I can't say anything connected with cars would be my weakness."

"Your mom's the same way," Howie replied. "Every time I meet her down here she complains about how she hates to drive."

"Runs in the family, Howie; the car culture down here drives me nuts, too, but hey, each to his own. I'm glad you're having fun with it," Julie said sincerely.

Julie really liked Howie; he was a kind, caring man. On one of his conference trips to South Asia he'd gone out of his way to meet her in India to give her a salami he'd toted along at her mom's suggestion. It had proved a very welcome change from the local vegetarian food she'd been eating for weeks.

"So it sounds like it's going okay for you, Howie, but apart from zipping around town in your hotrod, do you like being retired?"

"You bet," he answered without hesitation. "All my friends up North ask me 'whaddya do here, it's so boring.' I have a great answer; I even got a T-shirt made with the slogan: 'I used to be tired, now I'm retired.' A lotta guys, it's true, fill in the void with busy work, doing stuff around the house, gardening, cutting out discount coupons for the supermarket. It doesn't sound very meaningful, but it helps structure the days, I guess. Some folks start traveling, you know, in groups—not my thing, but why not? Some of the hobbies these retired folks take up, like Internet gambling in these new gaming cafes, seem to me like a waste of time, and money, too, but people find different ways to enjoy their new lives."

"It's not like where I worked in India, Howie," Julie said. "In Hinduism, there are four stages of life. The third stage is, I guess, what we would call retirement. But in India people ideally view that as a time to abandon all worldly desires and social ties and wander in the forest seeking nirvana.

So many of the Indian men I met were looking forward to retirement. For them, that's when life begins."

"I thought life begins when the kids go to college and the dog dies," Howie joked.

"No, I'm serious, Howie. In fact, that joke sort of proves the point of the contrast. In America, when people feel they have no more responsibilities, that's the time they can begin to enjoy themselves and engage life, including its social and material dimensions, more deeply, kind of the opposite of India. Maybe we could learn something there, especially now that medical technology is extending old age so substantially. Retirement could last twenty, even thirty years. That's a long time to spend in gaming cafés and Publix."

"Theoretically, I agree, Julie, but we've got our own culture, and it's not easy to change people's attitudes, though this whole eastern philosophy thing, with yoga and tai chi, attracts a lot of the retired folks. It's not for me personally, but I'm really okay with how things are going. I've got a few friends who came down here, too, and it's good to be able to see these people I've known for over fifty years. People think Miami is just all old Jewish people, but there's a lot of diversity. Sit by the pool for a few minutes and you hear Russian and Yiddish, yeah, but also French from the Canadians and a lot of Spanish. And they're not all retirees; there's still a lot of working stiffs with families here. The politics of our condo board is the same as everywhere: fights over everything, and you know from the university, the smaller the stakes, the bigger the fight.

"Of course, there's a down side to Florida. Did you ever look at the papers here? Their idea of fun events are support groups for cardiac and heart problems, cancer, osteoporosis. You wanna go to a 'marvelous Monday'? How about a senior survival workshop or an 'erase your mind, regain bladder control seminar'? Oh, sorry, that's just for men . . . anyway, you get the picture. I shouldn't make fun; more folks I know down here are dying off—stroke, cancer—I don't have to give you the organ recital. I scan the obituaries and hope I won't see anyone I know. Myself, I'm feeling pretty fit, Florida living is definitely good for your health, and I try to spend time contemplating my life rather than thinking about death. It's been a good life, too, with few regrets. I've been doing some column writing for the local paper. That's a dream I've had for a long time, you know, hoping I can still shape the world a little, sharing some of my ideas, and reaching a wider audience than I ever could as an academic. I never wanted money or power or celebrity—which is a good thing, I guess, since I never got them, but living here has a lot of satisfactions."

"I'm so glad to hear it, Howie," Julie said. Then looking at her watch, she cried, "Oops, time to go, I'm going to stop off at Grampa's for their delicious cinnamon buns—can't get those anywhere else, not even in New York. And I'm buying one of their fabulous shrimp salad sandwiches for the plane. All those folks eating their $3 pretzels will be so jealous." Julie gave Howie a big hug, wished him well, and walked downstairs, checking her watch again. *Just enough time to make it to Grampa's and fill up the tank within ten miles of the airport.*

She drove, as usual, at a little less than the speed limit, in spite of all the honking behind her to move it up, and soon came to Grampa's, just as she remembered it, on the corner across the street from a run-down shopping mall. As usual, most of the parking places in front of the restaurant were filled—even on a weekday. *On weekends, forget about it.* In addition to her cinnamon buns and shrimp salad sandwich, she bought two Jewish ryes— the best in South Florida, or all of Florida, for that matter—one for her mom and one for her sister. As she returned to her car, she noticed that, although the streets behind Grampa's, off Federal Highway, comprised a low-rise black neighborhood of private homes, and that the customers coming out of the downscale supermarket were all black, there was only one black customer in Grampa's. Black folk were still largely invisible in white areas in Florida, she knew, even when their neighborhoods were spatially close. The two populations seemed to patronize different stores and restaurants, occupy different worlds.

Back on the road, Julie put her thoughts about Florida's cultural diversity on hold as she concentrated on the route to the rental-car return. Although she had arrived at Miami, she had decided to leave from Fort

Lauderdale and didn't want to miss her turns. At the airport terminal, she nonchalantly wheeled her carry-on bag through the gate as carry-on luggage, though she knew it might be couple of inches over the limit. She'd packed the ryes in the small plastic Grampa's bag, hoping the gate attendant wouldn't make her pay extra for it. If she did nip her for it, maybe she could bribe her with a couple of slices.

No such luck, though. The ticket clerk called her back and insisted she pay the $20 surcharge for checked luggage. "Okay, okay," Julie said, "but this is really an outrage." The woman shrugged as if to say, "who cares," pointed to where Julie had to check the bag, and turned to the next person in line.

The plane was full, but Julie had an aisle seat next to a skinny person, and the flight left right on time. She didn't need a blanket or a pillow but fumed that the airlines were now charging for such amenities. *Forget it; think positive.* She'd saved a book for the flight, a new murder mystery about the culture of South Florida called *Boca Knights*, and it didn't disappoint. She read it with great interest and many laughs at the wisecracks of the lead character, a crusty ex-detective from Boston, only taking a break to eat her shrimp salad sandwich. On exiting the plane, Julie thanked the crew waiting at the door, saying with a smile, "That's what I like, a flight with no excitement." The crew chuckled back at the allusion, remembering the recent, thankfully unsuccessful, attempt of a terrorist to set a New York-to-Detroit plane on fire with a dud bomb hidden in his underwear.

Chapter Ten

Exiting the terminal, Julie felt energized just to be back in the city, observing all the folks from different countries waiting for their friends or relatives—no one in New York except immigrants had people meet them at the airport. She punched in the previously arranged car service number on her cell and waited outside in the central lane as directed. She was enjoying the sunshine, though the weather report had threatened snow for the next few days.

Surprisingly, when her car appeared, rather than the usual Panjabi or Pakistani driver, whom Julie always amazed with her perfect Hindi (or less perfect Panjabi), this man was Chinese, a Mr. Li, or maybe Mr. Peng. They carried on a pleasant, informative conversation—in English—about the different order of first and last names in China and America until he deposited her safe and sound at her Chelsea apartment building. She tipped him generously as he lifted her carry-on and knapsack from the trunk and opened the door to her building. Breathing a sigh of happiness (and a little relief, too), she whispered "home again" to no one in particular. Jeanie, the building's resident lobby sitter, wearing her Grandmothers against the War T-shirt, greeted her with a warning, "You have a good tan, Julie, but you know what the doctors say about too much sun and skin cancer." Julie smiled halfheartedly. *Typical senior citizen—always looking on the bright side.*

Pauli had left her apartment spotless as usual, with a spike of messages on her desk, her mail in her Trader Joe's shopping bag, and a container of his mother's vegetable lasagna in the fridge. *Great! No bother with dinner tonight.* She dropped her stuff and made a quick call to him, leaving a message of thanks for taking such good care of the apartment and "the Chairman," as he'd nicknamed her cat. "When I see you at our next aerobics class," she added, "I'll fill you in on my trip. There's a lively gay scene down there, lots of dishy guys, it's ve-r-r-ry hot!" She then left messages of her safe arrival with her mom and her sister. Mike wasn't at his desk at the precinct, so she just left a call-back message, noting that she'd be in the rest of the day and evening, and hoping they could meet for lunch or dinner before she got tied up in the new semester.

After unpacking her suitcase, shoving her clothes in the hamper, and emptying her backpack, Julie made herself a cappuccino. She sat down at her dining table for the serious work of finalizing the syllabus for "Death and Dying," her new cross-listed course. She incorporated some of the notes she'd worked up in Florida so that it reflected her own interests in culture and society. The course was taught in alternative semesters by the anthropology, sociology, and psychology departments, and for the next two years, anthropology would have its turn.

Walter, her department chair, had given her strict instructions: "Make death come alive, Julie. We really need to keep up the enrollments!" At first, Julie had resisted adding the course to her schedule, but upon reflection, she decided it was a good opportunity to experiment with a possible new direction for her future research. With all her visits to Aunt Lottie, the brouhaha about medical reform, and the growing importance of medical anthropology, maybe an examination of aging, death, and dying in the context of American culture was right on target. The anthropology of North America was a growth industry now as fieldwork abroad had been curtailed by the economic meltdown, international terrorism, and lots of little wars around the globe that had put interesting countries off limits. This might be the perfect time for a change.

Julie had chosen a wide range of topics for the course that she hoped would generate spirited discussion. Since in her view, denial of death was central to American culture, she anticipated that her younger students might not have thought much about the subject. Aunt Lottie's friends were always complaining that their adult children and grandchildren found it a "depressing" subject, one they generally avoided, even when it focused on necessary financial, medical, or funeral plans. "It's a reality, after all," the old folks griped, "but no one is interested except us!" *And I'm the same,* Julie chastised herself. *Didn't I just resent Jeanie for her accurate, plainspoken remark about my tan? Like most Americans, all I want is upbeat stories about aging and death, like that new TV program showing the elderly—no matter how atypically—hang gliding or rafting down the Amazon.*

Julie now recalled something she'd read by Ian Buruma, one of her favorite authors. In contrasting the fatalistic Japanese view of aging and death with the American rebellion against fate, Buruma had suggested that the attempt to stop time, to be always young, itself leads to a kind of death. To stop the process of decay is to stop living. The umpteenth facelift, the short skirts wrapped tight around the withered thighs—that could be viewed as America's typical response to impending death. Yet, like Buruma, Julie also saw something grand about the American rejection of fatalism. It gave people a thirst for experience that drove them in all sorts of adventurous directions.

But some of her older students, Julie believed, or those from immigrant families, who were already caring for their elderly parents, might energize her class discussions with their personal experience of her topics. Over the past year, even the mass media had featured the politics of health care reform, especially euthanasia and treatment of the terminally ill, generating high interest, intense discussion, and violent disagreements about it. Unfortunately, too, especially for her inner-city students, death by violence was not just an academic aspect of American culture. Many of them could probably put a human face on her syllabus issues like street violence, drug overdoses, and even capital punishment. The academy was no longer immune. Mass killings on an army base and at various college campuses was only one aspect of the recent violence in supposedly protected environments. The ivory tower itself had been galvanized when some professor gunned down the members of her P and B (Personnel and Budget) committee who voted against her tenure.

Julie continued listing additional topics that could expand her course beyond the usual: climate change and the dying environment; America's gun culture; Islamic suicide bombings, including the relation of martyrdom to terrorism; and death by diseases caused by corporate greed, like cigarette smoking and mountaintop mining—she remembered a colleague once telling her, "America is a gold mine; the corporations get the gold, and the workers get the shaft." Then there was medical malpractice and hospital environments that were implicated in unnecessary deaths much too frequently. She would relate all these topics to culture throughout the course, applying socioeconomic and cross-cultural analysis to the ways people thought about death and dying, both what caused it and how they responded to it. She would bring the perspectives of medical anthropology to all these topics. Even in the arts, death was big these days. She inked in a field trip to one fascinating exhibit she'd seen at the nearby Museum of Art and Design and another at an Asian art museum that compared death ritual in Tibetan Buddhist and medieval Christian cultures. *No problem making death come alive in America*, Julie concluded.

When Walter had looked at her syllabus, he'd shaken his head with a faint smile. "So political, Julie. Remember, this is a course on culture, not politics."

"Walter, come on, you know everything is political, especially culture, and especially the topics in this course. You can't tell me violence, illness, death, medical culture, and all the rest of it isn't political. Look at the work of Paul Farmer, that wonderful medical anthropologist who works in Haiti. He not only sets up health facilities for the poor but also writes about how the political and economic inequalities that deprive them of medical resources are a form of war against them. I want my students to know about anthropologists like that. They need to see how power and culture interact, and how this affects their own lives and their thinking about illness and death. I guess you could say I want to disorient them, get them to think about things in a new way, gain a new awareness. Anthropology itself is becoming more engaged, or activist, or public, or political—whatever you want to call it—so really the course is right in line with where the discipline is going."

Walter sighed and conceded. "Okay, Julie, I'm sure you'll do a great job. And I *am* grateful you agreed to teach the course. Just try to rein yourself in a little on the politics, okay?"

"You bet, Walter," Julie agreed meekly, crossing her fingers below the desk. "Consider it done."

As she finalized her syllabus with Walter's admonitions in mind, Julie was delighted to hear her phone ring and see Mike's number appear. "Hey, Mike," she said warmly, "perfect timing. How'd you manage with my being away for a month?"

"Not easily," Mike laughed. "Let's get together. What's good for you?"

"How about lunch in the new Chinatown food court in Flushing?" Julie replied. "I've wanted to go there for a while, and this may be a good time before I start teaching. We could meet at the stationhouse tomorrow about noon and walk over from there. Does that work for you?"

"You're on; I'll see you then." A pause. "Um, should I wear a nametag? Maybe you forgot what I look like?" he laughed again as he closed his phone. *Not in this lifetime!* Julie grinned contentedly to herself. Their first meeting had started out inauspiciously, in an interview at his precinct desk in Queens, where she'd related some information about a murder in India that connected to an extradition case of his own. His impassiveness, even severity, then, had thrown her off balance. But now his austere profile and hooded hazel eyes only reminded her of her favorite Florentine Renaissance portrait at the Met of a young man whose tilted face communicated a wary intelligence and supreme confidence at the same time. *Hold that thought*, Julie told herself. She pushed away the syllabus, zapped Pauli's lasagna in the microwave, dropped a few morsels in Chairman Miao's dish, and settled in to eat and relax with the rest of *Boca Knights*.

Julie enjoyed the subway ride out to the far reaches of Queens. The area was a fascinating ethnic conglomerate, one of the most culturally diverse zip codes in the United States, and that was reflected on the train. She felt so relaxed on the uncrowded subway after a month in South Florida, gripping a steering wheel with all her senses alert just to buy a quart of milk. As she approached the precinct house, one of the brick and brownstone beauties from the turn of the century, she spied Detective Charlie Geraci, one of Mike's close friends, also of Sicilian descent, leaning against a parked car and smoking one of his "light" cigarettes. His open cashmere dress coat and highly polished tasseled loafers made no concession to the frigid weather and portents of snow. "Great tan, Julie. You're looking very fetching," he said.

"Apt word," Julie preened a little. "Thanks. My mom brought back the hand-knitted beret and mitten gloves from Peru. Now come on, Charlie," she chided him after a warm inquiry about his wife and two kids. "You're still smoking those 'lights'? Haven't we had this discussion before? You know light tobacco is no protection when you inhale so deeply."

"Yeah, yeah," he replied sheepishly, flicking his cigarette into the gutter. *Another example of the denial of death that Americans are famous for*, Julie noted but didn't say out loud. "That's better," she asserted primly. "Now let me ask you a question related to a new course I'll be teaching. Do you know anything about the elderly incarcerated?"

"Yeah," he laughed at the description. "I know that rapist you helped Mike and Rajiv put away last year will be the 'most elderly incarcerated man of the year' by the time he sees daylight, if you can wait that long."

Julie smiled. "Cha-a-a-rlie, I'm serious."

"Okay, okay, I'll give it some thought. Hey, here comes Mike. I gotta say goodbye. Somebody has to earn the taxpayers' dime."

As Charlie ambled back inside the stationhouse, Mike jogged down the steps toward Julie with a big smile on his face. Unlike his friend, Mike was sensibly dressed in a utilitarian down parka and sturdy low-topped boots. "Mmm, Julie, I missed you." He hugged her tightly.

"Same here," Julie replied. "I'm counting on your coming with me next time."

When they had walked the few blocks to the Asian food court and settled themselves at a table, Julie began by saying, "I'm really glad to be back, Mike. It was a good trip: Aunt Lottie is all settled in an ALF, the weather was okay, and I didn't get into any car accidents, or 'incidents' as the media call them down there, trying not to scare off the tourists. And I'm thinking about something I want to run by you."

"Fire away," Mike said. "I'm all ears."

"So," she continued, "with my book on Indian marriage published and my promotion to associate, I'm thinking about my future research: what I should focus on and where I should go. My idea is that maybe for the next couple of years I should concentrate on studying American culture, instead of running off around the world."

"Hey, it'd be wonderful for me to have you close to home, Julie, but I don't know, do Americans have a culture you could research? That doesn't seem obvious, not like India or New Guinea or those other exotic places you anthropologists have put on the map."

"An often-asked question, Mike. I remember once talking about American culture in my anthropology class, and one of my students asked me if I meant California! But seriously, I think the answer is *yes*. There *is* a unifying American culture that also includes a lot of different cultures, or subcultures. Take the culture of South Florida where I just was. Mostly people there share core American values, but, mmm, maybe they place different emphases on them, or act them out in different ways because of their demographic. I thought about that all the time I was there. People say South Florida is New York's sixth borough, but actually it has a culture of its own."

"Florida culture?" Mike raised an eyebrow. "American culture, maybe I could buy, but isn't South Florida mostly just old people?"

"That's what most people think, Mike, but it's far from accurate," Julie replied, "though it's true that age segregation plays more of a cultural role. Even the Gold Coast gay scene is more age segregated. A friend of mine in his fifties told me he went to a gay bar down there and was the youngest guy in the place. South Florida includes lots of different ethnic cultures, too, like Haitians and Latinos—and not just Cubans—but even these groups play out their values differently there than in the rest of the country. There are socioeconomic classes peculiar to South Florida and, of course, the important retirement and medical communities that don't exist in most of the United States. And then there's the car culture"—here Mike interrupted her with a laugh, "Julie, now cars have culture? Can I get a grant to study that? I'm hankering for a new Mercedes."

"You probably could, Mike; I'll show you the ropes," she joked. "But see what I mean—it's how people think about cars—how that's tied up with status. After all, you said 'a Mercedes,' not 'a Chevrolet'—there's a reason for that. And rules of the road . . . you have to see the South Florida express-way system to truly appreciate how central cars are to people's lives there. The Gold Coast culture is really a microcosm of American culture, not just the values related to aging and retirement but so many other American cultural values, too. Look at the whole mortgage foreclosure thing, Disney World, the drug culture, and the financial scams and frauds, just like Wall Street—no coincidence Bernie Madoff had a home in Florida. There's even an organized environmentalist culture. Florida started with a dream, and the American Dream is a major reason people come down there. Not just rich people, either. Lots of losers float down here, homeless people, beach bums, dropouts, and white kids from the South with no skills who wind up unemployed without even the rent money for a cheap room. But still they come. I think Florida's a natural for ethnographic research, Mike. With Aunt Lottie, her friends and neighbors, and her new ALF, I've got a built-in community of informants. And I've got friends there all over the place I could hook up with."

"Maybe you're on to something, Julie," Mike conceded. "You know, I was actually down in South Florida once, a couple of years ago, in connection with a complicated custody case. I took a few extra days and spent them with the Miami detective involved, a Cuban guy named Ernesto. He filled me in on the whole area. There was some Santeria related to the murder, pretty weird, at least to me. The photos of the crime scene were a real education. Ernesto took me around to some of the Miami-Dade community outreach programs—very impressive; I wish we could afford more of those. He and his family were so hospitable; we still keep in touch. I really liked the place. Maybe not Margaret Mead in Samoa but pretty special anyway."

"There you go, Mike. And speaking of Margaret Mead," Julie added, "she was one smart lady. In a film I once saw about her work, she pointed out that it's much harder to study your own culture than to study some exotic culture far away. I'm paraphrasing here: 'It's easier to be a *cultural relativist* when you're studying cannibalism in New Guinea than when you're studying local politics or religion in your own hometown.' That always stuck with me. I agree with it, and this might be my opportunity to view American culture as an outsider, get a new take on things. That's really what anthropology is all about, in a way, exploring other cultures so we can become more aware of our own."

"Case made, Julie. Go for it," Mike assented enthusiastically. *And that,* Julie determined, *is exactly what I'm going to do!*

Chapter Eleven

Florida, mid-April 2009

Lillian sat up comfortably in the hospital bed she'd had installed several years ago and thought contentedly about her day. Her two dogs, Ike and Billy, were sleeping happily in their basket at the end of the bed. *Poor dears*, she thought, *you've had a hard day . . . a long walk with Angela; wasn't that nice?* Lillian was glad that her instinct about the teenager down the hall had been correct. The girl had asked about the dog walking because she needed the money and had promised to be punctual and reliable. She was a little shy when Lillian had introduced her to Ike and Billy, but she soon petted them gently, and they responded by yapping and dancing around. So that was settled. *That's what it is*, Lillian thought, *you have to give people a chance.* It was like when she had joined the WASP. She was thrilled to have the chance to serve her country like the boys she knew. The military didn't want to give the women that chance, and thought they were just dainty little misses who couldn't do a man's job. *But we showed them! Just like these newcomers will show us. Who cares if Angela's family just took in her youngest aunt with her tiny baby? So it cries a little. If they can live with it, why should anyone else care? Why, when I left the WASPs and Al and me just had that tiny apartment on the military base and we had Linda screaming her head off half the time, people understood. You did what you had to do, and things got better and you moved on.*

Lillian felt so much more relaxed now that she had taken her pain pill preventively. *Dr. Galbinki was right*, she thought. He'd told her that, if several nights in a row the pain got too bad, she could take the pills on a different schedule. "Try taking them before the pain hits you," he advised, "then in about twenty minutes you'll feel the relief and be able to sleep for a good long stretch." She'd tried it and it *had* worked. If she took a pill around 8:00 p.m., by 8:30 or so she'd be really dozy, and by 9:00 she'd be out like a light. She'd sleep maybe five hours or so, and then she'd wake up naturally, without the stabbing pain that was like a knife in the back. So now, even if she had no pain, she'd take a pill every six hours, and it seemed to be helping. She knew not to take more than four pills a day. Dr. Galbinki had been very stern about that. She glanced over at the bottle on her night table and saw she'd need another supply soon. Maybe she'd call Dr. Galbinki in the morning and he could drop them by or send a prescription to her pharmacy. She'd have a neighbor pick them up; Angela was probably too young for the pharmacist to trust her with such strong pills.

Lillian had always figured that the back pain was something from her old WASP days, and lots of girls she kept in contact with from the old days of flying thought the same. One thing everyone agreed on was they would never have exchanged those flying days for anything, back pain or not. She liked to hear from the gals who were still alive—*now that's a dumb way to put it*, she thought. *I couldn't hear from the ones that were dead, could I? But they're alive as long as we remember them, dead but alive*, she amended her notion. *Now there's an interesting idea to talk about with Lottie on our next phone call.*

Her nostalgic mood was prompted by a black-and-white photograph she had laid out on her bent-up knees and was peering at intently. There they were, the three "mousequeteers," Alice, Flo, and herself, trim and good looking in their WASP flight uniforms: sheepskin-lined leather Eisenhower jackets zipped up to their collars with silk scarves tucked in and baggy flight pants stuffed into the wool-lined half boots they wore on duty. *No hats, just their cropped, curly locks pushed securely back from their foreheads so they could get the job done right. Rusty, that was her, because of her hair color, and Alice, the brunette, and Flo the gorgeous blond who had quit a chorus line to enlist. She sure had the looks for it.* All of them had huge smiles on their bright young faces as they leaned saucily against one of those clunky, old two-door cars of the forties: round, dented fenders; humpy trunk; and small, uncomfortable seats. *Boy,* she laughed a little. *I sure wouldn't fit in a car like that these days.* It was swell of Alice to have her granddaughter copy the photo she'd recently discovered in the attic and send it on to her. Her own daughter Linda would love it. Maybe Angela would know the best place at the mall to have it copied, maybe blown up to 8 × 10. Linda had always been so proud of her mom. Lillian couldn't count the essays that girl had written about "My Unusual Family" and "My Brave Mom," all through school and even onto college. They'd always been close. *Al was a wonderful dad, of course, and we both loved him dearly, but Linda saw me as something really special. What a nice thing to go to sleep on.*

Adjusting the bed to the sleep position, Lillian turned off the light and threw off the covers, enjoying the warm April air coming through the slightly opened windows.

Maria Gonzalez shifted her crying baby from her left to her right shoulder and grabbed the key to the entrance hall door from the pocket of the plastic baby bag that was slung over her back. *Ai Dios!* She was in such a hurry she dropped the key and had to bend down to pick it up from the floor, which made the baby cry even louder. What if that old Mrs. Krauss, whose apartment was right inside the lobby door, woke up and came out to make a fuss? *What a* rezongon *she is.* "What is the English word for her?" she'd asked Luis. "Someone like her is always complaining to Gert, the landlady." "Grumpy," he'd told her. "Just try to avoid her." But every time she saw her, even if the baby wasn't making a fuss, the old lady would give her the evil eye. *What if she calls the* policia? *They'll find out I'm illegal and deport me.*

Maria tried so hard; she worked two jobs so she could contribute a little bit to the household, but with carfare and the babysitter, she was doing all she could. She knew things were tight with Luis, his wife, and Angela, and her staying there made it even worse, but what else could she do? They were her family and never made her feel bad about staying there, but she knew it had to be a problem. Soon maybe they could get her a room somewhere else, but for now she was stuck and had to make the best of it.

Maria put the key in the lock of the lobby door and turned it carefully, then shoved open the door as far as it would go with her shoulder and crabbed in sideways, trying to shush the baby. As she passed through, she turned to pull the door shut but saw a tall, thin, nicely dressed *Americano* enter after her, pocketing the key he already held in his hand. *Some rich relative of one of the other tenants*, she guessed, *staying overnight for a visit. If he tells his mother about me and the baby, they'll be out in the hall in a minute to complain.* Giving him a brief polite smile, Maria was happy to see he wasn't even looking at her but seemed to be searching for something in his pocket. She walked past him as quickly as she could down to Luis's apartment at the end of the hall, keeping her brother's door key ready in her hand. As she turned around to shift the baby again while she opened the door, she saw the man quietly enter the third apartment on the opposite side. Gracia Dios, *it's not Mrs. Krauss's door*, she thought as she shut her own door behind her.

The tall man slipped quietly inside the door he'd opened and stood silently in the darkness for a moment. Duplicating the apartment key had been easy; several extras had hung on a hook in the kitchen where the practically bedridden woman couldn't see him when he made the cup of tea he sometimes took with her. Even without a light, her big hospital bed was clearly visible. He stepped softly over to it, studying the large bump of the person who lay there, the covers thrown back, the heavy breathing noise of a medicated sleeper reaching his ears. He noted the sleeping dogs at the foot of the bed with satisfaction. He'd timed everything just right, with his advice about rescheduling her pill-taking times. Then he reached into his jacket pocket and brought out a syringe filled with succinylcholine, a relaxant that was given to patients with severe pneumonia to admit a breathing tube. The lethal dose the syringe carried would mean an unpleasant death. *Not my concern.* Once injected, the patient would be awake but unable to call out. That suited him just fine. *And they'll have to spend a lot of time and money to find any traces even if they do an autopsy. And why would they? She's old, for God's sake; she'd fought in World War II! And her back pain is legendary. And if those damn dogs wake up*, he thought maliciously, *I just might give them a shot of sux, too; that would shut them up forever.*

A room full of useless, selfish creatures, he reflected, readying the injection. True, she wasn't the worst of the Florida widows he knew—all of their husbands gone to their reward—the wives had made sure of that—while they enjoyed the fruits of their pensions and insurance policies. This one couldn't prance around in expensive clothes and enjoy social outings at her dead husband's expense, but she sure knew how to milk the taxpayers with her free medical care, prescriptions, special equipment, and transportation to hospitals—all courtesy of the U.S. government, which people like him were keeping alive with their hard work.

He pulled the cap off the syringe, but in his distraction, it fell to the floor. Although it fell noiselessly, it was still worthwhile to try to find it; but, first, what he came to do. He leaned over the bed and found a nice soft spot behind her bent knee where the needle mark would be all but invisible unless you were looking for it. He jabbed it in with the macabre thought—he admitted it to himself—that now she would really be dead to the world. He shifted her knee slightly so the site of the pinprick was flat against the mattress. Then, without even glancing at her face, he knelt down and scrabbled around the edges of the bed and as far under as he could reach for the cap. But he couldn't find it. *Forget it*, he thought, *it'll have no meaning by the time they find her.* He took a last look around and noted with envy, as he had every time he visited, the several glass-fronted cabinets displaying her collectibles. *I have to admit, the old gal had enough sense to pick this junk up years ago when it went for a song. It may be worth a fortune now.* He sighed, *what a damn waste.* Sticking the syringe back in his pocket, the tall man opened the front door of the apartment and looked both ways before exiting. *Do I know my customers?* he chortled to himself. It was his father's favorite saying. *Dad, that poor, dumb slob.* He supposed he ought to be grateful to him for saving his hard-earned pennies to send him through medical school. *But who could respect a man like him?*

As the man walked slowly over to the nearby mall in the warm, almost sultry air, he ruminated on his father and his mother and the life they'd led in America. It was the American Dream alright, for all of them, just not in the conventional way. His father came from a crappy little Balkan town, one day Serbian, one day Croatian, one day Albanian, one day Romanian—who knew, who cared? As a teenager, his father had lost his whole family when the town was destroyed beyond repair. He was lucky that his father had a friend in America, an Albanian who followed the traditional Albanian principle of *besa,* the obligation to protect people who need protection. So this man took on the burden of the ugly, gangly orphan his father had been after the war. The man gave him a bed and meager board, telling him that, if he worked hard, he could achieve the American Dream. And that's just what his father had done. He'd sold junk cosmetics door to door from a market basket—*can you believe it?* he asked himself even now. There was no item too small to sell and no profit too small to make. His English was horrible, even after years in America. "But there were two things I will never sell," he told his son, "my honesty and keeping a promise." *What a crock,* the man thought as he laughed aloud, *besa, honor, all those old traditions—no room for that in the gospel of wealth.* He recalled his father telling about the days he'd walk in a downpour to return some money someone had given him by mistake or the time he'd practically gotten pneumonia taking some selfish old crone—his words, not his father's—some junk to put on her face so she'd look nice for her granddaughter's wedding in the middle of winter.

But to everyone's surprise, his father had prospered, and the market basket was put away for a small shop, which he called—what else—"The Market Basket." Now the relative thought it was time for his father to marry and set up his own home. He called on a friend from the old country who had another friend, who lived up in the Bronx, in New York, where there was an Albanian community. "I want a girl from the home country," his father had specified, "someone who can work hard with me and have healthy sons that are real Americans." *The old man got a lot more than he bargained for*, the tall, thin man reflected sardonically. The girl turned out to be beautiful, peasant shrewd and a harder worker than his father ever could have dreamed of. They had him, the one son, who was badgered by his parents to live up to their every notion of a successful American. His father's ideal of honesty didn't come off so well, but his mother's ambitions for the good life shaped his character. His father's business prospered with his mother as an outstanding model of his cosmetics and the fashionable clothing they later carried in their store. *There were more stores but no hugs and kisses from "Mom," that loathsome American word applied to every woman who gives birth to a child, no matter how badly she treats it.* His father made sure there was money put away for college and medical school for him, and there was still lots more of it for his mother to spend: fancy dresses; a much more imposing house and finer furniture than their Albanian savior had; and extravagant social occasions that his father avoided but for which the charming, successful American son let himself be trotted out to like a thoroughbred horse. His mother stuck her nose in the business thoroughly, setting up a successful clothing factory to which his father was relegated like a slave. She was a witch, no question about it, and then, to top it off, she divorced his father, got a huge settlement, and his father was accommodating enough to drop dead—just like that, right in the street. But the dead come alive with an inheritance, and his mother became a Florida widow. The tall, thin man didn't take her telephone calls. He was the payment for her American Dream, and now he was paying her back.

Julie was grading papers when the telephone rang. She didn't recognize the number, and when she picked up, an unfamiliar woman's voice said, "Hello, Julie, this is Linda Rosen. You probably don't remember me, but

I'm the daughter of Lillian, your Aunt Lottie's next-door neighbor. We met a couple of times when we were both visiting Florida."

"Of course I remember you, Linda. I was just visiting Aunt Lottie in Florida and naturally we went to see your mom. In fact, my aunt just called me and told me that she died. I can't believe it; I know she had been in a lot of pain, but she said Dr. Galbinki was on top of it. I guess she was more ill than we thought. You know, she never complained."

"Well, that's what I'm calling about, Julie. You know Gert, the landlady? She used to sometimes check on Mom and has a key for emergencies. Last week, when she went to visit Mom, she called out first, like she always does, and when Mom didn't answer, she went into her bedroom. She found her lying peacefully in her bed, but she was dead, and her dogs were nowhere to be seen. Of course, they called Dr. Galbinki right away, and he came over and signed the death certificate, certifying 'natural causes.' When Gert told some of my mom's friends, they were kind of surprised, I mean it's true Mom was in her eighties, and she was ill, of course, but still, it came as a shock. I spoke with Dr. Galbinki on the phone, and he told me he had visited Mom that morning. 'She probably had a heart attack,' he said. That didn't seem right to me either; one thing Mom did have was a good heart. Anyway, there's some other stuff that happened that I would really like to speak with you about in person, if you could spare the time. I know you live in Chelsea; I'm not too far from there, and we could meet whenever is convenient for you."

"Absolutely, Linda. Is it okay if I bring along my friend Mike? He's a detective, and he might have something helpful to say, but only if you don't mind."

"Not at all, Julie. In fact, I think that's a very good idea."

Julie called Mike to find out when he was free to come into the city for lunch and called Linda back with a time and place.

They met at one of Julie's favorite restaurants, East of Eighth, where you could linger for as long as you wanted over lunch. As she and Mike waited for Linda at a table by the window, Julie recalled the important things that had been discussed here in the murder and rape cases of two years ago, where she had played a small role in helping Mike and his partner put away some very bad guys.

Linda saw them immediately and walked over, extending her hand to Mike even before they were introduced and then giving Julie a big hug. After scanning the menus, they signaled to the waiter. When he had taken their orders and left, Linda looked at Julie and Mike and said, "This whole story is going to sound unbelievable, but everything I'm telling you is true. I've been over it so many times I don't even have to refer to my notes."

Julie had already filled Mike in on Lillian and her friendship with Aunt Lottie, and how the landlady had found her dead and called Dr. Galbinki. "Linda," Julie said, "why don't you take it from there."

"Well, of course, I arranged for the funeral," Linda began. "You know my mom was buried in Arlington Cemetery; your aunt probably told you about that. Most of her friends from Florida couldn't come, but there were a couple of her old WASP buddies there, some already in their nineties. When I first spoke to that Dr. Galbinki I told him I was flying down immediately and would meet him at the Comfort Providers Funeral Home; that's where her body was sent. When I met him, he very strenuously suggested a vault cremation, and I almost went berserk. I really lost my accountant's cool and screamed at him that she was going to be buried at Arlington and immediately told the assistant director to hold her body until I could complete the process for her burial there. I called her lawyer to make an appointment to see him, and he told me to come over as soon as possible in regard to my mother's will. When I got there, he showed me a will that had been messengered over the day my mom died. The new will had my mom's signature on it, but it was not her handwriting. The will was badly typed, and the witness signatures were practically illegible. It didn't have any reference to her substantial bequests to the WASP Museum in Texas or to Veterans for Peace, or more importantly, the stipulation that she was to be buried in Arlington National Cemetery. My sister and I got the remainder of the estate, except for this outrageous bequest to Dr. Galbinki of all her collectibles. I know that's not possible, because she had promised them to her grandchildren who used to love to play with them—very carefully—when they came to visit. I can't believe she changed her will so drastically without telling me about it. I asked the lawyer if he knew who the two witnesses to the will were, and he said he didn't, so I tracked them down myself from the real estate office that handles the building. One was a Cuban neighbor who hardly spoke English, and the other was the maintenance man for the building. Both of them told me that a tall, well-dressed man came to them the day before my mother died and asked them to sign some piece of paper. I'm not paranoid, but I think Dr. Galbinki gave them a few dollars to sign the fake will. Then he forged my mom's signature and murdered my mom that night. Partly, the problem is that there were no wounds or bruises on her body, so I didn't really know what to do. Do you think you and Mike might help me figure it out?"

"Let me think about what I can do, Linda," said Mike. "Maybe I can run Galbinki's name on some of our special computer databases. Many surprising things surface when people turn up dead."

Chapter Twelve

"*Death and Dying*, Mike," Julie cajoled Mike over the phone. "How does that strike you for a couple of hours this Saturday?"

"Can't we do something a little more lighthearted, Julie? I get all the death and dying I need on the job."

"This is just death and dying *virtual*," she wheedled. "I want you to see this museum exhibit with me in connection with my Death and Dying course. It's the Rubin Museum in Chelsea, a comparison of death in the East and the West, Buddhism and Christianity. I'm sort of at a disadvantage since I'm neither a Buddhist nor a Christian, and it would be really helpful for me to get your response. It would prepare me for the kinds of questions my students might ask."

"Okay, Julie, but payback is you have to go with me to the Mets game; they're playing a subway series with the Yankees, and you know how I love to see the Yankees lose."

"It's a date then, two dates actually. Pick me up at noon, and we'll walk over to the museum together. They have a lovely café where we can have a bite afterward."

"We'll see about that, Julie. This stuff might make me lose my appetite."

Julie and Mike were greeted in the museum lobby by two grotesque, larger-than-life-sized statues of contorted Mongolian "Lords of the Charnel Grounds." They wore fierce death's head masks in the form of skulls, with gaping holes for eyes, bared fangs, and a crown of skulls atop their bony foreheads. A large sign above them featured the exhibit's name, *Remember That You Will Die: Death across Cultures*, which was echoed in the glossy brochures Julie and Mike held in their hands. "Okay, I'll remember," said Mike, only half-joking. "Let's get started."

Though Mike wouldn't admit it to Julie, he found the exhibit fascinating and the descriptions printed on the oversize wall cards provocative. Now Julie directed his attention to "Lords of the Charnel Grounds" directly in front of them. These male and female skeletons with oversize skulls occupied a place in Buddhist culture that Mike found totally foreign. They belonged to the culture of Tantric Buddhism—he was startled into recognition of the phrase, though he couldn't quite recall why—and had a function he found bizarre. Charnel grounds were the places where dead and often mutilated and decaying bodies were disposed of, and where yogis went to meditate as a way of learning to confront death. These skeletons were their protectors. *The dead protecting the living from the dead?* Mike wondered. Like Julie, he always carried a little notepad, which he now took out of his pocket to write down the question. Julie smiled a little in satisfaction.

"One of the exhibit themes is the similarities as well as the differences regarding death in the European Christian and Tibetan Buddhist cultures," Julie said, as she pointed Mike over to another wall poster. "Both cultures use graphic and frightening images of death to motivate people to act virtuously in life."

"The Buddhist images are certainly graphic, Julie. I can see Buddhists are big fans of skulls and skeletons. But then," he added, "I guess Christians are, too. Look at this Victorian pocket watch, with a cover in the form of a skull. 'Time waits for no one and our stay on earth must sometime come to an end,'" he read the message aloud. "It's an awesome accessory, Julie, but don't even think about buying me one for my birthday. I'll take a regular old Patek Philippe, you know, the gold one without the skulls."

"See, Mike, I knew it would be helpful to have you along. That's just the kind of comment I expect from Alexander, our class comedian," Julie retorted, her mouth breaking into a smile. "Like you, he's really very bright and thoughtful, but like most Americans, his preferred form of denial is humor, especially in reference to death. I bet anything he'll have some smart remark about rock bands with this next display." Julie led Mike over to a trumpet made out of a human shinbone and a set of drums made from a male and female skullcap. "Remember the yogis in the charnel grounds. With these instruments, Buddhist yogis deliver the same message: 'life is impermanent and death is our constant companion.' These are the kinds of similarities, maybe even universal cultural themes, that I want my students to think about."

"And here's another similarity, Julie." Mike stopped before a woodcut of death in the form of a skeleton grabbing hold of a medieval peasant on his way to market. "Death as the great equalizer. Whether you're a pauper or the pope, no one lives forever. We see that in the job all the time." He paused for a moment. "But, you know, the big question for me isn't the equality of death. That's a given. It's the inequality of lives that's the issue. My guess is that, with the lousy life so many people on earth live, death is a welcome introduction to something better."

"A great point for consideration." Julie made another note in her little moleskin notebook. "Hey, maybe you could sit in my class as a ringer. You could wear your jeans so low your underwear sticks out and sling your baseball cap sideways and ask a few questions if the discussion stalls." As they moved on to some depictions of hell in medieval Christian imagery, Julie followed up on that thought. "Seriously, though, Mike, what *do* you think? Is there a direct connection between the quality of people's lives on earth and their views of death and an afterlife? Judaism, for example, is a religion largely based on rules for right living, the 'law' of a thousand details of daily life. Even orthodox Jews don't spend a lot of time thinking about heaven and hell. Not the way Christians do."

"You might be right, though I only know about modern evangelical-type Christians from the popular media. But when I went to Catholic school, some of the more old-fashioned priests were into those pictures of the Last Judgment and the tortures of hell just like these Buddhists. I've seen lots of those paintings: very vivid, the punishments the devils hand out to the sinners; they're way beyond just scary—monstrous demons literally eating up the sinners, sticking whole bodies into their gaping jaws. I wonder if anyone's done psychological studies of what's behind these symbols. Can you scare people into good behavior? I don't know. Statistically, serial killers or mass murder profiles include some folks with a very strict religious upbringing. So maybe the scare thing backfires."

Julie nodded her head thoughtfully. "But see, that's a big difference then. Even though both religions try to frighten people into good behavior, Buddhists also see death as an opportunity to achieve enlightenment. Their meditation practices prepare the person for death, yes, but also for what follows, a *cycle* of rebirths until one reaches nirvana, the end of the cycle when you're no longer reborn. Hindus, too, of course. I remember once encouraging a Hindu friend to take a risk on something by saying with good old American optimism, 'you only go around once.' 'Not in my religion,' he answered back. That gave me pause, Mike. You know my dad was a scientist, a truly good man in every sense, but his morality didn't come from a belief in any afterlife. His favorite line to help me make a difficult decision was 'life is not a dress rehearsal.'" Julie made another note in her book. "Using lines like these for comparison/contrast essays would have to provoke student response, don't you think?" she asked Mike.

"I do," he affirmed, "not that any of my Catholic school teachers would have ever promoted—or even permitted—such discussion. I guess, like you, I came to my beliefs through my parents. They sent me to parochial school for a solid foundation in the 3 Rs, not the theology. But don't you think that it's mostly people like us, the privileged few, who can afford these beliefs, Julie? Medieval Christians, slaves in America, and sick or poor people the world over—why wouldn't anyone with a miserable life want to have an eternal afterlife of heavenly bliss to look forward to? It's their great escape. And speaking of escape, any chance of our moving on to something a little more upbeat?"

"Okay, okay," Julie smiled, "how about sex and death? Did you look carefully at some of these Tantric bronzes, the Lord of the Dead in what is obviously a sexual embrace with his consort? Remind you of anyone?"

Mike paused for a minute. "Fleagle, that serial rapist we put away. I knew the phrase sounded familiar. Weren't his websites full of this Tantric stuff? Well, he'll be way past sex by the time he gets out."

On an unseasonably cool May afternoon, Julie awaited her students outside the Museum of Art and Design, where a field trip to a new exhibit, *Dead or Alive*, was taking the place of her class meeting. She had used some of her notes from her discussion with Mike on the Rubin Museum exhibit to explore cross-cultural themes of death and dying, and the students had seemed interested. This new show of contemporary art was even more provocative, disturbing, and nightmarish in certain ways. The exhibits, mainly created by younger artists from Western cultures, raised questions directly relevant to the students' own lives and would hopefully provoke the students to formulate their own ideas about the art, which had multiple meanings.

Julie reminded the students to take notes on their reactions to the exhibit, as these touched on questions about life and death, and reminded them, in response to a question, that the material would indeed be on the midterm.

Exiting the elevator, Julie gathered the students around a platform that displayed a human hand, foot, and skull that appeared lacy and delicate. "Take a close look," she encouraged the group, "and think about what you're seeing here. What materials has the artist used to make these sculptures? The exhibit title, *Dead or Alive*, may give you a clue."

"Looks to me like some kind of grass or feathers, the way it's woven so delicately," volunteered Adriana, one of Julie's best students.

"Good guess, Adriana," said Julie, and a few students nodded their heads in agreement. "But it's not grass, and it's not feathers. These sculptures are made out of dead cockroach legs and wings glued and woven together."

"Yuck," said Amy Stoddard, from the back of the group. "Dead cockroaches! That's disgusting. Why would anyone want to handle dead cockroaches to make art? And anyway, is this thing really art? It's just an imitation of a human hand and a foot and a skull."

"But it makes you think, actually," Adriana spoke up again. "We all hate cockroaches, but they do kind of relate to human beings. They exist in huge populations all over the world, and they'll eat almost anything to survive. Maybe that's the connection the artist wants us to make."

"Good for you, Adriana," Julie said warmly. "In fact, that *is* one of the connections that the artist, Fabian Pena, makes in his art. He's also honest enough to admit that cockroaches are cheaper than paint." That got a laugh as Julie led the students to the next exhibit, a group of skeletons of extinct birds. Before they had a chance to look closely at the sculptures, Julie asked how many of them had ever eaten fried chicken at a fast-food restaurant. Almost all the students raised their hands. *I guess the vegetarian thing hasn't quite caught on here*, Julie thought, *but this might make them think again.* She then explained that these were sculptures of birds that had been driven to extinction by hungry humans, and they were made from chicken bones disposed of by fast-food restaurants. "Is it a kind of recycling, maybe," Julie asked, "making the dead chickens come alive in the artistic representations of dead birds, birds that are gone forever? Is the artist sending a message about throwaway food and throwaway species?"

"Pretty weird," offered Alexander, nudging his friend Zeke and shrugging, "but I do sort of get the point. Is this the kind of stuff you're going to want us to write about on our midterm essay?"

"Exactly," Julie smiled slyly. "Try to get past the 'weirdness' and open yourself to the questions and emotions the art provokes about the fine line that divides the living from the dead. Think especially about how the materials are so unexpected and how the artists use them to make a point."

As Julie led them to the next exhibit, a big Harley motorcycle completely covered by a cow's skeleton, called *Mad Cow Not Edible*, she said, "On my visit with my aunt in Miami this winter, I actually met the artist, a woman named Billie Grace Lyon," noting how the feminine noun had gotten the group's attention. "She was driving the bike around South Beach, stopping to talk with various people. She was even letting them take photographs of themselves astride the motorcycle. My aunt asked her what did she 'mean' by the whole thing," Julie continued. "'Well, one interpretation,' Billie Grace told us, 'is that the cow is something slaughtered to fulfill human needs, and it keeps on working after its death as art. Maybe it will provoke us to think about how our dead, both human and animal, no longer return to a natural integration with the earth, so we need to find different uses for what's no longer alive.'"

This conversation had reminded Julie that she should include a couple of sessions on tissue and organ transplantation in her syllabus. There were huge controversies about those processes, and organ donor organizations tried to convince people in their advertisements to donate so that they could give the "gift of life." Of course, unlike this art exhibit, the whole theme of death was repressed in the field of organ donation, another part of death denial so prominent in American culture.

Julie then led her class to the final display she'd earmarked for their attention. It looked fairly benign after the chicken bones and the cow skeleton. A mound of powdery-looking fluff piled on a cube was placed adjacent to a loom with a lovely woven tapestry in it. "What's this supposed to be?" Alexander asked, and then wished he hadn't.

"This," said Julie dramatically, pointing to the mound of fluff, "is the skeletal remains and fur of mice that barn owls have eaten, digested, and regurgitated because the bones and fur are indigestible. The loom's tapestry is woven from thread spun from the mouse fur."

"This is so gross," said Sita, who was from an Indian family, and perhaps a vegetarian, but most of the students in fact nodded their heads vigorously in agreement. "Don't tell me there's a message here, Professor Norman."

"But indeed there is, Sita. Something pleasing, that invites our touch, has been woven out of something 'gross' as you say. Might this suggest that there is nothing in nature so 'gross' that it may not be put to some productive or even beautiful use? Or we might ask, why is regurgitated mouse fur *repulsive* but coats and hats made of ranch-raised mink or the fur of seals captured in the wild a status symbol for some people? Or is the artist alluding to something else entirely, perhaps a religious belief that the soul and even the material body rise to a higher form of life if they have fulfilled their duty in their earthly life?"

"And now," Julie said, "I'll let you explore on your own. As you do, think about the material on death we've discussed in class. I think you'll find this exhibit provocative, and some of you may even want to return with some friends or your families." "Yeah, right, that's what my mom wants to look at, owl pellets and cow skeletons," Julie heard Alexander's stage whisper and the laughter of the students around him.

Julie opened her e-mail and immediately scrolled down to the one from Mike. Hers was a "CC" actually addressed to Linda. "Hey, Linda and Julie," it read. "I did run Galbinki on the computer and found some references that will certainly interest you. He'd moved around to several different hospitals, no reasons given except in one case where a family had made a formal police complaint and forced the hospital to investigate. But in the end it fell apart and Galbinki resigned, claiming innocence and false accusation, which he had every right to do. Me personally, I believe the old saying, if it looks like a fish and it stinks like a fish, it's a fish, look no further. But in fact, I've had cases that wound up just the opposite and the fish that stank was a little teddy bear that got railroaded, and it took us a long time to find that out. But Linda, I definitely think you're onto something. When you return to Miami to settle up your mom's apartment, I want you to call my buddy Ernesto Cruz who leads an elder abuse squad down there. I'll give him a heads up; here's his cell number."

Chapter Thirteen

The man with the limp hurried down the hospital hallway to the room he had checked out beforehand. It was going to be a good night for him. A three-car smashup on I-95 a week ago had resulted in four young male bodies being brought to the hospital: the perfect candidates to bring his quota up to date—*Lotta pressure, lotta pressure*. He had talked to their families about donating their organs, but the kin weren't quite ready to sign up yet. Even with all his talk about how this would be a way for the boys to keep on living, their parents still hesitated. He didn't like to get too aggressive; this was capitalism at its best—the demand would never outrun the supply—but the whole field was getting crowded and competitive, and harder to control. It was a big business now, and the public was starting to get involved, making quilts and websites for their dead relatives, insisting on making donors known, and getting publicity. *That was all wrong.* This business depended on anonymity: *no names, no names.*

As the man quietly entered the room where one of the young accident victims was on a ventilator and held a pillow over his face, he felt he'd earned some good luck for a change. Young men whose heads had been smashed in car or motorcycle accidents were the best kind, especially if they came from middle-class families. They were more likely to be in good health, and their organs weren't spoiled by drugs or alcohol. And if they hadn't been to prison, their bodies were usually AIDS and cancer free. *Jeez, some places are really hitting the bottom of the barrel, using prisoners and even lying about the diseases they had.* Things had gotten a little easier with improvements in medical technology, and the constant demand for product made the over-sixty crowd a little more acceptable. But, still, Miami didn't have that big pool of the "knife and gun club" folks like they did in some inner-city areas: victims of urban violence and illegal immigrants; maybe he ought to think about going where the pickings were easier.

His work completed, he returned to his car, hunkered down, and called a private number at the funeral home from his cell. "Another delivery tomorrow morning," he said. "I'll be there around midnight, and my guy will be waiting out front to deliver the stuff to the airport in time for the 3:00 a.m. flight, no problem. Make sure you have it ready, and don't forget my cut."

At midnight the next evening, the man with the limp drove to the funeral home, and the funeral director came out, carrying a satchel of money that he placed in the open trunk of the man's car. He then carried some big freezer boxes to the waiting van and returned back inside, shutting the door, never speaking a word. The limping man waved the van driver over, gave him a stack of bills, and said, "Get moving, but don't mess up. Drive under the speed limit; you know where to go."

As the limping man drove off up I-95 to his apartment, he reflected that maybe all good things come to an end. *This is getting too dangerous*, he thought. *That FBI case up in Brooklyn might be contagious. And there's no way Mr. Funeral Director is going to carry this weight alone. Okay, so real estate tanked, but I still got the pain clinics; drugs are always steady cash. Maybe I can even make a killing at the casino. Too bad Lou didn't turn out to be a guy I could tap for a few bucks; what a wimp: takes his winnings right to the bank and wouldn't part with a nickel.* The man gritted his teeth and made the decision—*I'm outta here, maybe even move to a different part of the country; guys with my skills don't grow on trees.*

It was after midnight. Manuel sat in his van waiting for the man he had arranged to meet outside the funeral home to pick up a "delivery." *Delivery of what?* Manuel wondered as he nervously thought about this part-time job he picked up recently. *Gotta be something illegal,* he guessed, but he knew better than to ask any questions. With the economic downturn, he was desperate for the money but thought maybe it was time to look for something else.

As Manuel drove off to the airport, he considered the whole deal again. *That guy, Mr. C., he's too hinky. I'm gonna make this my last trip, even though I need the money. It's not right what they're doing, disrespect for the dead. I'm going to call the* policia. After dropping the packages at the airline terminal, Manuel pulled up short at a public phone just before getting on the highway. He said, "9-1-1: tell the Miami Police to check out Comfort Providers Funeral Home; there's some stuff going on there that you want to know about." Before the operator could ask his name, Manuel hung up the phone and got back on the expressway. *America has been too good to me,* he thought. *I can't do this thing.*

Back in the small town in Guanajuato, Mexico, where he was born, Manuel's father was a farmer, who just about kept the family going. As a teenager, Manuel moved to Salamanca, a bigger city where there was more work than in the countryside. He even graduated from high school and got a job as an industrial painter and sandblaster back in his hometown. But there was no real future there. After a year, he headed North, like so many other Mexicans, in hope of working across the border. It had been a hard and dangerous crossing into Arizona after the long trip from Salamanca, crammed into an old van with other young men like himself with the same ambitions. It had cost him a bundle, but he saw it as an investment. With what he could make in America, he could send money to his family to build a house and help bring his brothers here.

He worked for a year in Arizona, but things were getting hot for illegals there, what with the new border fence and increased vigilante action. A couple of men he had crossed with had already been discovered and deported, and some had even been killed by a vigilante group. Manuel took a big chance when he decided to return to Mexico after a year—another dangerous journey—but he wanted to marry his *novio*—and then she got pregnant. Manuel again decided he could do better finding work in the United States and paid a coyote $2000 to bring him across. But he wouldn't stay in Arizona. He hooked up with a bunch of guys going to Florida, where he heard there was more work and less harassment and the climate was good. Again, he made a long journey in a van jammed with guys like himself. When they got to Florida, someplace near the ocean they called the Gold Coast, the driver just dumped him and the others. Manuel was lucky, though. Friends of friends found him a small place to live, and he got a job as a roofer, and then another job painting houses. From his first paycheck, he sent money back home; in those days, he used Western Union or a money order, but now he felt safe enough to do it through a direct payment from his bank. *Not completely safe, no.* As an illegal, he couldn't take any chances. Florida hadn't yet become crazy over deporting illegals, but everywhere people were getting antsy because the ICE enforcement was becoming more intense. *All I need is to go over the speed limit or pass a red light, and I'll be back in Mexico in a minute.* Everyone he knew was becoming afraid to leave their houses now, but he had to work or else how could he help his family?

And he had prospered. The streets of the Gold Coast weren't exactly paved with gold, but with hard work and saving his money, even with the money he sent back to Mexico, he was doing okay. He made friends with a Cuban gardener working in one of those upscale condo communities, and when the guy had to quit his job, he offered it to Manuel. The lady he worked for was *una muy buena senora*; she never treated him mean like some of the other ladies, or just ignored him like he was invisible. And she spoke Spanish, too, and was a professor. She had even been to Mexico, and she had a beautiful garden that he loved taking care of. By keeping his eyes open, he learned the gardening business in a couple of months and just a year later was made foreman of one of the gardening crews. Then he decided to take a chance. He'd been working for somebody else for seven years—long enough. He bought a used truck and some used gardening equipment and went out on his own. His wife was living with his family where she had their first child, Alejandro, who was now fourteen. *Time to get them here*, Manuel thought, so he sent money for her and his son to come to the United States. They came the same way he did, a long, dangerous journey, but *gracias a dios*, they made it here okay.

They found a little house in Pompano Beach, a big Spanish community there, and the business thrived. But being illegal cost him. Some damn lawyer who swore he could get Manuel his green card took his $3000 and then said, "Sorry, I need your money to pay some debts of my own, and I can't help you anymore." *And who could I complain to? I can hardly bring my case to court!* A woman realtor he worked for and trusted sold him her home for a good price, signing papers with a lawyer that she would pay the back taxes and insurance she owed, but she never did, and Manuel didn't know it until the bank came after him for all the money. *Thirty thousand bucks gone in that deal.* So, like half the people in Florida, he had to leave his house and bought a trailer home in Pompano. *And I can't do a damn thing about it.* One wrong move and they could deport him. He couldn't let that happen. Some more bad luck followed: someone broke into his truck and stole all his equipment—and he couldn't do a damn thing about that either. Same as all his friends, what could they do except look for more work, whatever they could get. Some of the guys he knew who hung at Home Depot were offered ten bucks an hour by some nutcase just to stand with signs in front of some fancy condo place, but he wasn't that desperate—yet. But if things didn't get better, he might have to do it. He had three children now, and he had to take care of them. So when he had to go to the emergency room for an accident on the job, he jumped at the chance offered him by some guy who worked there to drive a van: easy money, he said. Manuel just knew it was trouble but took it anyway—*no options left*, he thought. But he wouldn't lose faith in America—or himself. *I love this country: it's still got great opportunity, and it's a better place for the kids—they're like Americanos now. The girls all have real American names, they speak English, they don't even have a Spanish accent any more, they're doing well in school, and you don't have to worry about some drug gang shooting and killing, and about paying off cops. I'm not going to give up,* he determined. *But this is the last time for this job. Maybe if the laws change, that immigration reform they're talking about, with amnesty I can get my citizenship papers. Then I'll finish building my beautiful house in Salamanca and go back there to see my family, bring over the brothers here legally. Just don't give up,* he told himself. *Take the bad stuff and keep on moving forward. "Dios te lo da y Dios te lo quita."*

🌴 Chapter Fourteen

Memorial Day weekend, Florida, 2009

The Miami Palms Nursing Home facility was quiet, though many of its beds were occupied. The rare visitors were usually gone by 8:00 p.m. Nurse Esther Mendelsohn came on at 9:00 p.m. and stayed until 5:00 a.m., a shift she preferred partly so that she could attend to some practical chores without interruption. But mainly, it was during the late night hours when many of the elderly, restless sleepers would lie awake for hours with no visitors and nothing to distract them from their pain or anxiety. It was in these deepest hours of the night that Esther could spend time with them, comforting and providing company at their bedsides, which was almost impossible during the busier daytime hours.

She saw Dr. Galbinki on his evening round, later than most doctors would come out, she knew, going from room to room to check patients' symptoms, their improvement or increased debilitation, and tapping his handwritten notes about each one into the computer that stood on a stand outside the nurses' desk. Around 10:00 p.m. he made his last visit, to Lottie Freund's room. She was a heart patient Esther was quite fond of, who could be optimistic and even funny at times, but who, in the last day or so, had become more frightened of the various symptoms she described and was talking of removal to the hospital.

Dr. Galbinki sat down by Lottie's bedside and asked her how she was feeling. His tone lacked sympathy, and she felt that. "I told you I'm feeling very lightheaded all day, not just when I wake up, and I can't breathe easily." He let her talk, hardly listening; it was the same complaints all the time, or rather, different complaints each day. He'd always given her more time than other patients, but she was taking advantage. He was tired of her whining tone, her recriminations that he wasn't taking her seriously.

"Don't be such a crybaby," he said to her unthinkingly now, as she added another symptom, loss of balance, to her litany. *Yesterday, it was weak legs; the day before, lightheadedness upon waking; and the day she came in, heart flutters—mideighties, for God's sake; do these Florida widows expect to enjoy their good life into eternity? Always me, me, me. They have highly paid caregivers who have no choice but to listen to their list of ailments, and if they're lucky, younger relatives who hang on their every word in hopes of getting something out of their wills. But that's never enough for them. The doctor is the expert, the one they really want to drown with their questions. Questions based on half-baked Internet sources, television programs, or advertisements, or worse yet, from friends whose aunt or cousin or cleaning lady has the same problems. They all have misinformation and criticisms to throw at the physician, his diagnosis, and his treatments; they've heard of someone who died from these things. Enough from this particular Florida widow.* Not the richest or the meanest, nobody could top his own mother in that department. But tonight he was at the end of his tether with her. He'd stuck a syringe of potassium in his pocket, which he now felt for, and wrapped his hand around it.

"Doctor Galbinki," Mrs. Freund was saying, "I'm not a crybaby; that's unkind of you to say. I really am in pain."

"I know, my dear, forgive me; it hurts me to see you feeling so badly. I do hope to hear you're improved when I come by. Look, I take your pain so seriously, I'm going to give you an injection of pain medication a little stronger, with a little morphine in it to let you sleep through the night. You'll see how much better you'll feel in the morning. And if not, I've promised you, we'll take you straight to the hospital. Just lie back and relax." He found a vein in her arm to insert the syringe and waited for several minutes until her body went limp. He stayed several minutes more, knowing no one would enter her room, and then checked her pulse and breathing. None. He replaced the syringe in his pocket, arranged her legs in a comfortable sleeping position, and turned her face to the wall.

Running into Nurse Mendelsohn as he exited, he had to listen to her tiresome plaudits about herself, how she looked in on all the patients in the "wee hours" as she coyly put it, and if any were awake she would keep them company awhile. He cautioned her that Mrs. Freund was sleeping very deeply now; her pulse was okay and her breathing regular. "Please do not disturb her," he asked. "Peek in at the door by all means, but if she's still sleeping soundly, it's important for her well-being that she gets all the rest she can and awakens naturally."

Esther promised she would do exactly that. And what she promised, she did.

"Dead! How can she be dead?" Julie cried into the phone. "She sounded so well and happy at the ALF—" Julie sighed in exasperation as her mother interrupted. "Mom, that's assisted-living facility, acronym ALF, Miami Palms, remember? It had the nursing home facility on the premises, but in the back—oh, that's right; you weren't in the golf cart with us when Murchison pointed it out—so the ALF residents could 'age in place.'" Julie sighed again at her mother's query. "Nooo, Mom, that's not my description; that's what they call it in Florida . . . oh, never mind that now. Just tell me what you know." After listening to the few sketchy details, Julie's anger broke through her tears. "She died of natural causes—that's what they put on her death certificate! I don't buy it. I just talked to her last Friday; she was looking forward to my visit after the semester finished, and especially when I told her Mike might join me for a week or so. You know our diamond heart ritual; she'd never want to miss that." *There's stupid for you*, Julie berated herself, *as if Aunt Lottie had died deliberately to frustrate my plans*. "Look, Mom," Julie continued more calmly, "I'm going to call Charlotte back today and see if I can get more details from her. You have all Aunt Lottie's papers for the prepaid funeral arrangements, flying up the body, so why don't you call the funeral home down there, arrange for that, and then call the rabbi up here and reserve him for the burial. You know it has to be within three days; they'll get you someone, I'm sure. You call Jennie and any old friends of Aunt Lottie who might be alive—maybe the owners of the hardware store where she worked; probably they're dead, too, after all these years. I'll call Mike, and I'm sure he'll offer to come, but really, I'd rather make it small. I do not want to call Frankie and Arlene myself, but I suppose I have to. Or maybe Charlotte could do that, though I guess they'd be insulted. Don't worry about Lottie's old apartment; it's paid up for several months. When I go down in June, I'll settle that up. Let that odious Mrs. Murchison whistle for the maintenance for Aunt Lottie's apartment for now. You can bet I'll be talking to her. I have a lot of serious questions to ask those people. She won't fob me off with vague answers. Let's talk tomorrow."

Julie cleared off her dining room table, placed a legal pad and several pencils on it, and flipped open her cell phone. Chairman Miao snuggled in her lap, soothing her anxiety. *First, Charlotte. Try to get a factual, coherent story about what happened.* When Charlotte picked up, both anger and sadness clearly vibrated through the phone. After offering her condolences, the normally unflappable Charlotte explained that when Mrs. Murchison notified her that Aunt Lottie had died suddenly of "heart failure" and asked her to call Julie's mom, Charlotte had immediately asked for more details and questioned why Mrs. Murchison wasn't notifying Lottie's sister or Julie herself.

"She went on about how she'd tried but couldn't reach either of you and, of course, didn't want to leave a message with such news," Charlotte said, "but I don't believe a word of it." She then continued, imitating Mrs.

Murchison's mincing voice: "'And don't you agree, Charlotte, that as a dear friend of the family, they would appreciate hearing such sad news from you rather than me?' My foot," Charlotte continued, "she just wanted to get off the hook. You know, Julie, I don't like making trouble, but I just don't trust her. Dr. Galbinki's been okay, I have to admit. He visited your aunt a couple of times at Miami Palms, made sure she was settled in alright, made a cup of tea; you know how he could make himself at home for his important patients. I guess he sort of felt responsible for the recommendation. But you'll see him yourself when you come down to settle up your aunt's things, won't you?" Julie assured her she would and said she'd be back in touch.

Julie clicked in Mrs. Murchison's number and began somewhat ungraciously by stating that her mother had been quite distraught at hearing about Aunt Lottie's death through Charlotte's phone call. She had expected Mrs. Murchison to call her immediately, regardless of the time, about such an occurrence. "Obviously," Julie said, "Charlotte did not have any details, and my mother and I have many questions we'd like you to answer." The manager immediately went on the defensive and offensive simultaneously.

"You have my sincere condolences," she intoned, "and I tried to reach your mother and you, but I only got a message machine. Of course, I could never leave such a message, don't you agree?"

What can I say to that? "Well, now we're connected, and I'd like to know exactly what happened. Aunt Lottie sounded so well when we spoke only a few days ago."

"Well, my dear, your aunt *was* very elderly," Mrs. Murchison replied in the same bogus soothing tones Julie recalled her using in their tour of the facility. "She just died quietly, without pain, of natural causes, which is really the best way to pass on, isn't it?" *Ugh*, Julie thought disgustedly, i*sn't there any other way to talk about the elderly without such condescension, like you're speaking to kindergarten children?*

"Well, that's not for you or me to judge, is it?" Julie responded testily. "My aunt was one of those active seniors you mentioned in presenting the advantages of Miami Palms, wasn't she? If you can't provide me with further details, I will, of course, speak with Dr. Galbinki when I come down at the end of my semester. Perhaps he can make sense of this."

"Of course, my dear," Mrs. Murchison assented, "more than welcome. Dr. Galbinki was very fond of your aunt, and it was he who found her on his morning round and gave me the information that she had quietly passed away. But do make an appointment first. You know our excellent doctor has several different offices and is a very busy man."

Chapter Fifteen

As soon as Julie completed her calls to Charlotte and Mrs. Murchison, she called her mom to relay the news. Her mother said she would call the funeral home, Comfort Providers, to arrange for the prepaid funeral. "I'm just hoping everything is kosher with them. There's been some news articles about fraud in the prepayment funeral business; some of these guys take the money and run instead of putting it in the trust like they're supposed to. I'll let you know as soon as I call them."

"Okay," sighed Julie, "and I guess I'll have to call Frankie and Arlene. I know they'll want to be there, and they don't have much time to make it up here for the funeral."

Within the hour, Julie's mom called back and told her, "Everything is kosher. They'll send the body to the funeral home up here that is specified in the contract. All Aunt Lottie's wishes are spelled out clearly. They deal with a lot of Jewish people, so they know the rules: no autopsy, plain pine box, graveside burial, the rabbi for the graveside prayer, all within three days. The cemetery is the same one where Uncle Sol's family and Bobby have their plots, perpetual care, all taken care of. The funeral is set for two days from now."

Lottie's family plot was in a cemetery on Long Island, very near where Julie's own father and her grandparents were buried. Julie's mom had told her about the near fiasco when her grandfather had died. Julie's mom couldn't remember the name of the cemetery where they had a plot because her mother had died so long ago and Julie's grandfather had wished to be cremated, no muss, no fuss, no rituals, no memorials, no flowers, no nothing. Finally, her mom had remembered that the family plot was in a huge cemetery on Long Island where the Spanish Civil War veterans had been buried and asked the funeral home to find out where that was. When the assistant funeral director called back, he said there was no Long Island cemetery where Civil War veterans were buried.

"Not the Civil War," Julie's mom had corrected him with exasperation, "the Spanish Civil War!"

"The *Spanish* Civil War?" the young assistant director had echoed her phrase, hesitantly. "What was that?"

"I can't believe this," Julie's mom had said, restraining her anger. "You never heard of the Spanish Civil War?"

"Okay, okay," he said, "I'll look again," and finally he'd come up with the right cemetery.

No such problems with Aunt Lottie's funeral, Julie thought gratefully, as she phoned Frankie in Florida. Arlene answered the phone and told Frankie to get on the other line as Julie told them the news about Aunt Lottie. "Sorry for the short notice," she said, "but the funeral has to take place in two days. Do you think you can make it?"

"Of course we'll make it," Arlene answered with asperity. "And Tony and Mary Francis will be there, too; you know how much we loved Aunt Lottie. How did she die?"

"Well," Julie said, "the death certificate said 'natural causes,' but we'll never know the specifics unless we have an autop—" "No autopsy," Arlene yelled into the phone. "Jews don't have autopsies."

"Of course not," Julie replied. "there's no reason for an autopsy. I wasn't suggesting it. I was just trying to answer your question. We'll see you at the cemetery around noon."

Precisely at noon, on the day of the funeral, Julie, her mom, and her sister Jennifer arrived at the cemetery. Jennifer's husband David took the time off to be with Kai, who they all agreed was much too young to attend a funeral. Frankie, Arlene, Tony, and Mary Francis all arrived a few minutes later, suitably dressed in black, with sad expressions, mandated by the American cultural rules about funerals. They hugged Julie, her mom, and Jennifer but otherwise expressed no emotion.

Soon after, the rabbi appeared and the funeral ritual began. As the rabbi chanted the Hebrew graveside Kaddish, Julie's mind strayed to the importance of death rituals and the many they had for the grieving survivors in all cultures. The funeral ceremony served as the beginning of the grief and bereavement period for the survivors. It reinforced the integration of the family and the community and helped the survivors to begin their separation from the deceased through the process of mourning.

Death is universal, Julie ruminated, *and every culture constructed a set of beliefs and rituals centering on death, the body, and the fate of the human soul. These demonstrated the universal human preoccupation with dying and the decaying human body, even as actual ceremonies took on a very different shape in different societies.*

American rituals were unlike those in many other cultures, where death was viewed as a transition from one social status to another, and where it was believed that the dead remained in touch with the living, with the power to act for good or for ill. In those cultures, rituals honoring the dead and communing with ancestral spirits were constantly observed. Like the Dreamtime of the Australian aborigines, whose people believed that the ancestors created all the animate and inanimate things in the cosmos, including the aboriginal peoples themselves. In all important Australian ceremonies, the people re-created the Dreamtime through the telling of legends and ritual performances. In Madagascar, the living were brought into actual physical contact with the dead through dances performed with the shrouded remains of their ancestors' bones in a periodic ritual called *famadihana*.

The social and psychological functions of these widespread beliefs and rituals were not difficult to understand. Societies regarded themselves as ongoing systems, and the death of any member threatened their very existence. Perhaps that was why so many cultures refused to consider death an irrevocable end to life but rather the beginning of a new existence. Beliefs in an afterlife and linking death to resurrection were several of the ways to answer the threat that death made against the social system. Julie knew that the Western beliefs and rituals emphasizing the separation of the dead from the living stood in contrast to most other cultures where the continuity between the past and the present, the living and the dead, and the individual and the community were the basis of important communal rituals.

As Julie observed her own restrained emotions and those of the mourners at the graveside, she thought again about cultural differences. For Americans, outward "bearing up" and emotional self-control at a funeral were important values. The practice in other cultures of wailing and crying, or even self-mutilation by the mourners, seemed exotic and even shocking. Her students in her Death and Dying course had gasped as she described the funeral scene among the Warramunga of Australia, where some of the women lay prostrate on the body while others dug the sharp end of their yarn sticks into the crown of their heads, from which blood streamed down over their faces, all the while keeping up a loud continuous wail.

Julie emphasized in her class that, although death is the most intensely experienced of all human crises, it was the one least talked about in American mainstream culture, because of the anxiety surrounding it. This helped explain much of the advertising of the medical industry's public relations regarding the transplantation of organs and tissue, which used posters of plants and butterflies, symbolizing life. Any talk, at least in public, about the *processes* of organ procurement and donation was suppressed. Also central to American death ritual were memorials to the dead, like the many headstones she saw around her, which symbolized the American identification of life with individuality. These grave monuments—headstones with the deceased's name and abbreviated biography, dates of birth and death, and reminders of family relationships—"beloved" husband, wife, siblings, children—were important in restoring individuality to the deceased after the anonymity of death. In spite of the medical profession's attempts to deny the realities of organ and tissue donation by the emphasis on, indeed obsession with, anonymity of both donor and receiver, many relatives of dead organ donors forced the individuality of the donors onto the public stage, including, of course, on the Internet.

As Julie mused on these ideas, the rabbi's special burial Kaddish ended, and the mourners threw the obligatory handful of dirt into the grave. As they got ready to disperse, the rabbi chanted the special verse from Ecclesiastes for leaving the cemetery: "Then shall the dust return to the earth whence it came, and the spirit shall return unto God who gave it. Peace be with you, all whom death has united in this field, the last home of so many of our departed. Peace be with your souls, which have been recalled by the voice of God to eternal life. Amen." He then recited the Twenty-third Psalm, and their small group left the gravesite.

Because Frankie and his family were staying with relatives way out on Long Island and didn't want to make the long trip back into Manhattan, they had all agreed to dispense with the customary gathering after a funeral. While Julie's mom and Jennie stayed behind for a few moments to thank the rabbi, Julie walked off slowly to the parking lot, deep in her own thoughts. Frankie and Arlene caught up with her, and Frankie asked somewhat bluntly, "How did Aunt Lottie die, Julie? You didn't say exactly."

"I don't know," said Julie. "There was no autopsy; I guess it was just old age." She started to move on, unaware that Frankie and Arlene exchanged a look that conveyed *some unfinished business here.* Touching Julie's arm to slow her down, Frankie asked with an attempt to put an apologetic expression on his face, "Do you know anything about the disposition of the will, Julie?"

"Will?" asked Julie, turning to face him. "What makes you think Aunt Lottie made a will?" Frankie and Arlene exchanged another look, one that Julie read as both surprise and dismay.

"Well, we just assumed there was one," Frankie explained. "Maybe you know who her lawyer was; has someone gotten in touch with you about it?"

"Aunt Lottie didn't make a will, Frankie," Julie replied, "and I don't think she had a lawyer either. I'm going down to Florida as soon as school's out to settle up her apartment and do some checking around, and of course, if there's anything to tell, I'll be sure and get in touch." With that,

Julie hugged Arlene and Mary Francis, and she, Jennifer, and her mom entered the car that had brought them to the cemetery and drove off, leaving Frankie and Arlene standing alone, grim faced.

As soon as Julie got home, she called Mike and asked him to meet her at her apartment for dinner. "No problem, Julie; how'd it go?" Mike responded.

"Nothing I can't handle, Mike, but there's a bunch of things about Aunt Lottie's death I don't understand, and I'd really like your advice."

Early that evening her bell rang, and as soon as Julie saw Mike at the door, she embraced him tightly. She led him to the table, which held a simple meal of salad and baked chicken. "I'm so glad you could come," Julie said. "I'm very confused about Aunt Lottie's death, and it's not the kind of thing I'd want to talk about in a restaurant."

Julie began by telling Mike that the manager of the ALF said her aunt died of "natural causes." "Is that a legal cause of death?" she asked. "You hear so many stories about what goes on at these places for the elderly, and I haven't been able to contact Dr. Galbinki yet. I really want to talk with him and also to someone at that funeral home where her body was taken. At the funeral, Frankie and Arlene asked me about Aunt Lottie's will, and they seemed very surprised that she didn't have one. Then they asked about her lawyer, but I don't know anything about that either. I'm definitely going back to Florida to settle things up at the end of the term, and I was hoping you could come with me."

"Great idea, Julie. I have vacation time coming, and meanwhile maybe I could check out some of the cast of characters. You already know Galbinki didn't come out completely kosher on the computer database; maybe I could dig a little deeper. Who else should I be looking at?"

"Well, Galbinki for sure. I just don't trust that guy, especially after hearing Linda's story. And Aunt Lottie once told me in one of her phone calls that another neighbor of hers, who also used Dr. Galbinki, had died unexpectedly. Charlotte had worked for this woman also; maybe she can tell us something useful. I'll be seeing her when she comes to help me clear out Aunt Lottie's apartment."

"You don't suspect Charlotte of anything, do you?" Mike asked in some surprise.

"Oh, no, of course not, Mike, even though Frankie and Arlene always made snide comments about her. But maybe she knows something about Aunt Lottie's last days that could help set my mind at ease. And definitely Mrs. Murchison, the woman who runs the ALF. Maybe we could speak with some of Aunt Lottie's friends, too, like Lou"—"Yeah, Lou the saint," Mike interrupted sarcastically—"and maybe Gert, the landlady, will have something to say," Julie went on.

"Not a problem, Julie; I'll get on it. And I'll contact my buddy Ernesto in the Miami PD Elder Abuse Squad; I told you and Linda about him. I know his family will want to have us over for dinner, but I'll also make sure we get a chance to speak with him privately, and you can ask all the questions you want."

Chapter Sixteen

June 6, 2009

Julie bounced into the apartment and tossed the plastic bag containing her academic robe and gown onto the couch where Mike was sitting, his bare feet up on the wooden trunk that served as a coffee table. "So, how was graduation?"

"Really inspiring, Mike," Julie replied, hanging up the cap and gown in its plastic pouch. "A lot of the full profs don't even attend any more. It's too bad; it means so much to the students and their families—it's a long, tough climb for so many of them, sacrifices of time and money I certainly never had to make. And one of my students received a scholarship for the University of Miami's PhD program in forensic anthropology. The speaker was great, a former gangbanger from the Bronx who's now the principal of a public high school; he got turned around by that youth group, the Urban Dove, that helps kids change their lives. The audience really connected with him; the applause was tremendous. And he was bittersweet funny, too. I was wiping my tears on my sleeve."

"Sounds compelling; we all need that. Being a cop, I guess we see the underside—the ones who don't make it and *are* dangerous; don't kid yourself about that—but the cops I work with, Charlie and Rajiv and the rest, take this 'protect and serve' thing to heart, and it's good to see the news is not all bad."

After a quick lunch, Julie and Mike headed for JFK, where their flight left right on time. After landing at Miami, they retrieved their luggage and picked up the same little KIA at the same rental place that Julie had used in January. Even without a GPS, they found the time-share without difficulty. Their apartment was spacious, with two large bedrooms—well, they wouldn't need both of those—but each with its own bath (an unlooked-for luxury), a big balcony overlooking the pool, and a much larger kitchen than either of them had at home. On the counter was a sheaf of papers about the activities the time-share offered. "Look at this, Mike," Julie exclaimed, pointing with a laugh to the next afternoon's events. "In a place where most of the guests are at least forty pounds overweight, there's a 'Make Your Own Ice-Cream Sundae' and a 'Junk Food Bingo' only two hours apart. But hey, here's a Zumba class in the mornings. I definitely want to do that with you. You'll get a real kick out of it."

"Julie, Julie, can't I just swim laps, take some runs? Or we can take long walks."

"Forget walking," Julie retorted. "We're in Miami. Nobody walks unless you want to do the golf course, which is pretty boring after the first time. In case you didn't notice on the ride over, there're no sidewalks around here. We'll save our walking for South Beach or the Everglades; there's some beautiful hiking there. And don't forget, we have business to attend to. I have to settle up both of Aunt Lottie's apartments, dispose of her stuff to Charlotte—maybe she can give some of it to her church—and whatever she doesn't want, maybe Gert will take. The same for her apartment in the ALF. I want you to come with me to question Mrs. Murchison, the ALF manager, about Aunt Lottie's death. Since she died in their nursing home facility, maybe she can give me some specific information that wasn't forthcoming in our phone call. Then there's the funeral home, Comfort Providers—what awful names they have—that shipped Aunt Lottie's body up to New York. I want some information from them also. And Dr. Galbinki—we have to make an appointment with him. Murchison made a big point on the phone about how busy he is."

Here Mike interrupted: "You know, Julie, I wouldn't be in a hurry to let Galbinki know in advance that you're coming to see him. You might learn more if you take him by surprise. If he refuses to see you, you can always make an appointment for another day. And you don't have to introduce me as a detective either, just a friend, and let's see what I pick up that you might not."

"You're right, Mike," Julie agreed. "Sometimes I play too much by the rules; it's naive, and I need you to set me straight. That's the *only* reason you're down here, right?" she joked, giving him a big hug.

Julie took the wheel of the KIA the next morning for the ride to Miami Palms, explaining to Mike that she knew the way blindfolded from the "pilgrimage" she'd made to the ALF in January, and suggested he would find the neighborhood interesting. She had warned Mike that if Murchison picked them up in the golf cart with her poodle upright in the passenger seat, he wasn't to smirk. "Just try to play it like an ordinary guy, consoling me in my mourning period and helping me settle Aunt Lottie's affairs. We'll discuss everything in detail afterward." Mike promised.

"Smirking is an offense that could earn a cop a CD—that's a command discipline, like a demerit—from the inspectors—they call them 'the hounds'—who make surprise visits to the precinct houses to catch the cops off guard. Honestly, Julie, I just read in a *Village Voice* article about policing in the city that one smirk earned the whole borough of Brooklyn thirteen CDs. I would never smirk on duty." Then he smirked.

As Julie turned into the Miami Palms gatehouse, she noticed the same alert young man at the security booth who had been there in January. *Good for him; he's held on to his job, not easy with each passing month of rising unemployment statistics*, Julie noted, pleased. Julie told him that she had an appointment with Mrs. Murchison, and he picked up the phone to call her. After a moment, he told Julie and Mike to park by the admin building and that Mrs. Murchison would meet them there. *Too hot to ride us around in the golf cart with her poodle, I suppose*, Julie thought, glad to be spared that indignity. Mrs. Murchison was wearing the same wide-brimmed white mesh hat as last time—what Charlotte had called the "Hallelujah hat, like the ladies wear at our Baptist church," she had told Julie with a wink. Julie introduced Mike to the ALF manager, and they all sat down.

"We are truly sorry for your loss, especially in so sudden a manner," Mrs. Murchison told Julie. She sounded sincere, not an easy task when she probably had to say these same words to so many family members over the years. Julie wondered if perhaps she had judged her too harshly. "Her death had nothing to do with her residence here, I can assure you of that," Mrs. Murchison went on, sounding a little defensive. "We only have the finest people as residents, and our staff's references are very carefully checked. Your aunt had just moved temporarily to our nursing home facility at the behest of Dr. Galbinki, to whom she complained of a recurrence of her heart flutters. With her medical history, he wanted to keep her under his eye for a few days, which I believe showed laudable concern. Your aunt was very happy here," she continued, "even though she didn't make much use of our many excellent facilities or take her meals in our lovely dining room." The last comment rang in Julie's ear almost as a rebuke, reminding Julie of her earlier ambivalence about the manager. Once more, she put her warmer assessment on hold.

"I'm just here to understand exactly what happened," Julie asserted as she had in her phone conversation. "It's just so odd to me that, after Dr. Galbinki gave her a clean bill of health following her hospital stay, and so highly recommended your facility, that she should die here after only a few short months. We have a copy of her death certificate, of course. Dr. Galbinki certified her death as 'entirely due to natural causes,' that is, 'neither trauma injury nor poisoning.' Those are the only reasons listed on the form; he didn't actually list what those 'natural causes' were."

"Well, my dear, if one doesn't die of an accident or as a suicide—which has never happened at Miami Palms—one has to put something on the death certificate. Death is natural in its own way for the very elderly, isn't it? And going peacefully in *my* sleep is the way *I'd* like to go when my time comes," Mrs. Murchison concluded, affecting a soothing, reasonable tone. Mike, for his part, affected a look of mute thoughtfulness, which he turned Julie's way, signaling her not to say anything further. Julie moved on to the practical concern of settling up her aunt's apartment, saying that she and Mike would have a moving van at the ALF early the next morning.

"Is there someone here we can pay to move the few heavy things we might want to take?" Julie asked.

"You can ask our guard, Mr. Jefferson, at the gatehouse," Mrs. Murchison replied. "He's proved very helpful on such occasions and has supplied only reliable and trustworthy people so far. We've never had a problem."

"Thank you," Julie said, "we'll arrange it on the way out. Now, though, I would like to speak with the nurse at your nursing home facility who would have overseen my aunt's stay. Is she here, do you know?"

Mrs. Murchison punched her cell phone and spoke into it for a brief moment. "Yes, she's there now. Ask for Nurse Esther Mendelsohn. She was very fond of your aunt."

As Julie and Mike walked across the main campus of Miami Palms to the nursing home, Julie said, "Of course, Mrs. Murchison didn't mention homicide as a cause of death. I guess it wouldn't even cross her mind."

"I can understand why," Mike said. "Even a suspicion of a homicide would empty a place like this. A certifying doctor could—or would—probably never even contemplate raising that possibility unless some very fierce demands were being made by the family. Let's face it, these are the 'old old' folks; they're going to die sometime, and without a stick in the eye about the circumstances of the death and real evidence, the police, and certainly the DA, would not get involved. And Julie," Mike went on, "you did real good not pushing on this cause-of-death thing by saying you'd be going to see Dr. Galbinki. She would have called him in a heartbeat if she'd thought that."

Chapter Seventeen

Nurse Mendelsohn came out to greet Julie and Mike as soon as the receptionist paged her. Julie was surprised to see that she was a very old-fashioned-looking woman, maybe in her fifties, wearing what looked like a wig of shiny brown hair in a short pageboy and, despite the June heat, black stockings under a long, full skirt. It was an appearance Julie recognized as associated with the very religious Jews who now lived in many different communities in New York and its suburbs as well as in the Miami area. The nurse did not shake their hands, but she smiled warmly at Julie. "I know you have questions about your aunt's death," she said. "Let's sit in one of these private offices." She led them into a nearby room and shut the door. She looked somewhat askance at Mike, who pointedly hung behind Julie, sat farther away from the nurse, and did not look directly at her.

"I was very fond of your aunt," the nurse began, "and when she entered our nursing home facility, Dr. Galbinki explained to me she had a long history of hospitalizations for heart trouble of various kinds. He didn't feel that it was *too* serious this time—she had described 'flutters' and weakness, shortness of breath, an increasing loss of balance and lightheadedness when she awoke and during the day—but, of course, there could be complications. Dr. Galbinki recommended she remain here for a few days to see how her symptoms developed. As he is our 'on call' doctor, he saw her every day. After a few days, your aunt said she wasn't getting better and wanted to be moved to a hospital where they had advanced equipment and so on, but the doctor did not think that was necessary at this point. Now, I don't know if Mrs. Murchison told you, but in a personal religious way, I have taken a pledge to stay by the bedside of any patient in our facility whose death may be near, if they do not have friends or relatives close by. Maybe you know, Julie, there's a Jewish mitzvah, called *shomer*, a guardian, which can refer to a person who keeps watch over someone on their deathbed, as well as the body after death. I know from my experience as a hospital nurse for many years that dying alone is one of the great fears people have."

As she said this, Julie recalled her elderly neighbor who had died alone and was left for several days in her apartment, until a terrible smell forced Julie to contact the co-op board. They were in the middle of a meeting and insisted she wait until it ended before they heard her out. Julie was furious and called the police, who sent over an ambulance. There was no siren when they left; the poor woman had been dead for days. Julie turned her attention back to Nurse Mendelsohn.

"So, on the evening of your aunt's death," the nurse was saying, "I saw Dr. Galbinki on his round; it was about 10:00 p.m.—he is so busy with his office and hospital patients, you see, that he often doesn't get here until then. He's a very dedicated physician. I asked him specifically about your aunt. He already knew, for she had told him as well as me that she was feeling more frightened by her illness, that she might be close to dying, and that she wanted to go to her hospital. Dr. Galbinki did tell me that, while he felt your aunt's assessment of her condition was not accurate, he understood that a patient's psychology about her illness should always be taken into consideration. He thought her depression about her condition was just the normal fear of the elderly about death, especially understandable with her history of heart trouble. He told her that if she still felt so unwell the next morning, he would transfer her immediately to the hospital. It is true that your aunt told me she felt very anxious and depressed. Perhaps that caused the heart failure; that's what Dr. Galbinki suggested to me. And

he would know; that's his specialty, isn't it?" Julie disagreed with this diagnosis but remained silent. That's something she could take up with Galbinki, who she suspected would cover himself the way most doctors would.

"Then Dr. Galbinki told me that he sat with her for awhile until her
medication allowed her to fall soundly asleep. He made sure she was
comfortably positioned and emphasized to me how important it was that
she get a good night's rest. She was breathing deeply, with none of the
shortness of breath she had complained about, so he felt she would be fine
through the night. I told him I would just look in on her later—in case she
had awakened and wanted me to sit a spell at her bedside but that I would
be very quiet, just open the door and peek in and not disturb her if she
wasn't already awake. He said that was exactly right and thanked me for
my concern."

Esther looked at Julie compassionately and continued, "I did just what I
said, and I suppose I was the last person to see your aunt alive, comfortably
and peacefully asleep. So I can only tell you she died at some point in the
night. It was only when Dr. Galbinki returned for his morning round that
he found your aunt deceased."

Julie could think of no question that the nurse had not covered, so she
thanked her and rose. Mike left the room first, and Julie and the nurse followed, the latter waving goodbye as she turned down the corridor opposite
to the entranceway.

"Mike, here's my take off the top of my head," Julie began as they
walked back to the car. "I think she was quite straightforward, maybe a little enamored of Dr. Galbinki like so many of his patients are, but what else?
It's hard for me to second-guess Galbinki's diagnosis; he knew better than
anyone about Aunt Lottie's hospitalizations and surgeries related to her
heart condition. That's real. But he played it both ways: he didn't openly
pooh-pooh her symptoms, though it's pretty common that both doctors
and laypeople think that the elderly—and not only the elderly—exaggerate
their symptoms for a little extra attention. At the same time, he hedged his
bets. Let's face it, if he'd left her in the nursing home too long and she died
on his watch, that would make him look bad, so he *did* promise to put her

in the hospital the next day if she didn't feel better. That would cover his ass for any lawsuits about negligence, right? Nurse Esther's report about Aunt Lottie sleeping comfortably when she looked in confirms Galbinki's diagnosis. Then, okay, heart failure strikes her later in the night, and that's it: she dies; I mean, you do hear about people 'dropping dead on the back forty' all the time."

Mike had listened attentively to Julie and agreed that, although he had never met her aunt, based on all the stories about her Julie had told him, her analysis seemed plausible. But he was unwilling to let Galbinki off so easy. "Think like a detective, Julie, what *evidence* do we have that, when Dr. Galbinki left your aunt's room, she was still alive? Only this Nurse Esther's total acceptance of the self-serving little story Galbinki told her of how 'peacefully' your aunt was sleeping when he left her, how her regular breathing showed that she wasn't suffering from heart pains or whatever. He emphasized to the nurse not to disturb your aunt unless she was awake, and the nurse did just what he said, possibly partly because, as you noticed, and so did I, she had the conventional, old-style perception that a nurse is inferior to a doctor and never questions his instructions. I don't know if some feisty RN, like a few I've met on the job, would have been so quick to 'just peek in by the door' and wouldn't have tiptoed to the bed to see firsthand that the patient was breathing on her own. Don't get me wrong, Julie, I'm not faulting this Esther's compassion or even competence, but I can tell you this story wouldn't wash in my squad at home."

"So where do we go from here, Mike?" Julie asked. "We've got Linda's account of a forged will, which certainly casts suspicion on Galbinki, doesn't it?" she now asked Mike somewhat uncertainly. "Hey, Nancy Drew," he said affectionately but firmly, "*suspicion* is the operative word. It's true, when you compare the original will with the new one, it looks like evidence, but until we get the *proof* of the forged signature, and some other testimony, the investigation's not over by a long shot. And where's the gain for Galbinki, a bunch of kids' toys and piggy banks? And as for your Aunt Lottie, Galbinki and Murchison in cahoots? Will the ALF get fifty bucks more a month for your aunt's apartment? Is that worth killing her for?"

"No," Julie admitted in a small voice. "Of course, that's absurd. I don't know why; I just have a feeling that being at this ALF somehow killed Aunt Lottie."

"I'm not ruling that out, Julie; don't get me wrong. Maybe what we have to look for is a larger pattern. How were Linda's mom and your Aunt Lottie similar? Both were elderly ladies, very fond of Dr. Galbinki, but in some way did they set him off? Were they critical of how much money doctors made? Did they expect him to cater to them to the exclusion of his regular patients? Have there been similar suspicious deaths of elderly women, fairly well off, dying unexpectedly, who were Galbinki's patients? Maybe there's a psychological motive we haven't considered? We're going to see Ernesto in a couple of days. We can get him up to speed on Linda's mother and your aunt; let's see what he'll shake loose."

Back at the security guard's cubicle, Julie made the arrangements to have some men take Aunt Lottie's furniture from the ALF to her old apartment in North Miami. "Next stop, the Comfort Providers Funeral Home," Julie said as she slid behind the wheel. "I'll drive, Mike," she added. "That's back toward Aunt Lottie's old neighborhood again. We can grab a quick bagel lunch and then nail down a few more stops."

Chapter Eighteen

The Comfort Providers Funeral Home was almost straight back up north toward the hospital where Aunt Lottie had stayed in January. Driving in daylight now, Julie felt quite confident of not getting lost. She easily found the modest two-story white stucco building with a faintly antebellum portico, a few palm trees, and trimmed perpetual-care-type bushes at the entrance. Above the portico the name was written in stone. She parked in the small lot at the side of the building. Julie and Mike rang the bell on the front door, which was almost immediately opened by a youthful-looking, conservatively dressed man maybe in his midforties. He gave his name as Shawn Kean and ushered Julie and Mike to a long couch in a sedately appointed foyer. He seated himself in a chair opposite them, repeated their names after they introduced themselves, and asked how he could help them. Julie consulted a card she removed from her purse and asked if they could see the director, "a Mr. Beckett. We've come regarding my aunt, who died at Miami Palms Nursing Home at the end of May and whose prepaid burial arrangements, including flying her body to New York City, were made through your home."

"Actually, Mr. Beckett is not here; he won't be back today. I'm the assistant director, and I feel certain I could answer any specific questions you have about your aunt as well as any general questions you might have about her intake here. I've had a great deal of experience in the mortuary business both here and in Japan. But of course, you're free to come back to speak with Mr. Beckett himself if you prefer."

"Japan?" asked Julie. "I'd like to hear about that. How did that happen? I'm an anthropologist and would be very interested in your experiences there if you don't mind taking the time before we discuss my aunt's information."

"Not at all," Shawn said, seeming very pleased with Julie's interest. "You may remember that terrible earthquake that struck Kobe in the midnineties. The Japanese government was overwhelmed dealing with the thousands of people who were killed and asked for experienced American mortuary personnel to come over and help them handle the aftermath. Well, with my experience and academic qualifications—I have a degree in mortuary science from Miami Dade Community College; it's an excellent program—I was accepted right away. I was younger then, unattached, and quite physically fit, a real plus. I thought a year in Japan assisting in such a disaster would be doing well and doing good at the same time. One year turned into six! I tell you, the depth and variety of experience I got there I couldn't have gotten in a lifetime of directing a funeral home in the states. Plus, the new cultural perspective I gained on death and mourning was invaluable; it gave me a much broader outlook for working in the field than I ever would have gotten staying home. And it's even had some practical benefit as well. There are lots of different ethnic groups here in South Florida, and I've had quite a few occasions to put my cultural sensitivity into practice."

This is unreal, Julie thought. *Anthropology is everywhere.* Aloud, she asked, "What would you say are the chief differences between your work here and in Japan? Or maybe, are there more similarities than I think?"

"Well, the chief difference," Shawn responded thoughtfully, "is that, in Japan, cremation is customary, probably because historically there wasn't the space for burial. But of course, it also fits well with Buddhism's ideals about separation from the material world. And with reincarnation, as in Hinduism, fancy caskets and grave markers aren't required. I was a kid from a small town in central Florida when I went over there; nobody cremates where I come from. In America, the various religious and historical cemeteries are important to a lot of families because your burial ground and grave monument tell people who you were when you were alive. A box of 'cremains'—a combination of 'cremate' and 'remains' that we use for the ashes nowadays—on your home mantelpiece can't do that." He paused for a moment. "Actually, I bet a lot of folks in my hometown don't even know the word. I happen to think it's a very ugly one. I prefer 'ashes,' like the Japanese; that's what they are after all."

Shawn paused again, and then proceeded somewhat earnestly. "Obviously, many funeral directors prefer that people choose more traditional burials; it's better for business. Well, perhaps you'll forget I said that." He cocked his head at Julie and Mike, who nodded their understanding. "But the funeral industry has come up with a compromise solution that more and more people seem to find useful. They have wall vaults in cemeteries, like in New Orleans—have you ever heard of those?—for your container of ashes, and you can put a brief inscription on the stone facing outward. So it has the appropriate setting of a cemetery and a reminder of the deceased, but it's much less expensive. You pay by how high up on the vault your space is."

Like a New York apartment, Julie thought, and then asked, "So do many of your clients choose cremation, either with a simple container or a vault?"

"There *is* more widespread acceptance now," Shawn replied. "Partly, I think, because of the space issue, as in Japan, but also maybe because families are scattered more than they used to be. Many people realize that nobody will be visiting their grave anyway. Perhaps you know the anecdote of the woman who specified that her ashes should be scattered in the doorway of the local Target? That way she knew her two daughters would visit them frequently." Mike and Julie both smiled at the apt joke. "A little industry humor," Shawn said somewhat sheepishly. "I'm not making light of people's wishes. But, realistically, that's a factor, especially here on the Gold Coast where so many of the elderly are retirees from colder states a great distance away. And cremation *is* much less expensive than burials.

Younger relatives of the deceased, especially, have little familiarity with either death or its expenses. They sometimes consult with the deceased person's physician—who probably knows the deceased better than anyone else anyway—to advise them about what the person would have wanted, if there's no specifics in the will. I've found most physicians, being of conservative bents themselves, still opt for the old-fashioned burial, but some are quite modern in suggesting the cremains vaults.

"And, of course, in a few unusual cases where the family might have concerns about an abusive caregiver or hospital negligence, say, something like that, then burial would be the far wiser choice since cremation prevents any exhumation of remains for eventual investigation. In the bad old days, you could possibly prove a suspicious death by autopsy, because most common poisons like arsenic could be found in the blood. But such cases are exceedingly rare today. These popular true crime, forensic television shows, and whatnot, have made it pretty clear that only the most sophisticated medical person could get away with that kind of murder. Why, there's hardly any chemical anymore that you could put in a person's bloodstream that couldn't be detected if someone, or some agency, had enough interest and money to really pursue it. This doesn't pertain to your concerns about your aunt, of course; I'm just trying to cover all the bases for you."

Disarmed by Shawn's forthrightness, Julie told him that she had found his remarks very enlightening even if they didn't pertain directly to her aunt's death. "My aunt was quite elderly and had had several bypass surgeries, but she died unexpectedly in a nursing home facility, and all the death certificate said was 'natural causes.' I thought there'd be something more specific, like 'heart failure' or whatever. But her regular physician, Dr. Galbinki, who certified her death, said that that's how the death certificates are printed to read these days if there's no sign of 'poisoning or trauma injury.' I checked some death certificates in my family, and that seems to be true."

"Yes, indeed, Dr. Galbinki was correct there. I can only add to that, that if a person dies unexpectedly and unattended, without a clear cause of death, in many states that could warrant an autopsy. If the police are involved, of course, the autopsy is the medical examiner's job. But otherwise, autopsies are much, much rarer than people think. They're expensive, and unless the family is particularly adamant about it, they rarely take place. Especially for the elderly who die under a doctor's care, it rarely takes place, as was the case with your aunt, of course, who was being seen by Dr. Galbinki. With no autopsy required, that would leave cremation as a possible option. Did this come up with your aunt's case?"

"Oh, no," Julie replied, "She *was* elderly and did have a history of heart disease. And she was Jewish. You know I'm sure that Jews avoid autopsies unless there's some definite reason to have one, which there really wasn't in this case. I mean, there was no contesting of a will or foul play suspected. Well, it's probably just my disappointment that my aunt died so soon after starting a pleasant new life in a very comfortable retirement community."

"Now," Shawn offered, "may I ask if you were satisfied with our handling of your aunt?"

"Indeed, yes, it all went just as defined in the contract," Julie assured him. "Cremation was never an option. Her plot had been purchased next to her son and husband, the simple casket and rabbi all arranged in advance. So there was no discussion at all with Dr. Galbinki on that issue."

"I'm glad to hear that. I've actually met Dr. Galbinki several times, sometimes with family members of his patients. Most of them seem to place great confidence in him and trust his advice in these matters." Julie thought Shawn's pursed lips suggested some ambivalence at this statement. *Am I just imagining that?* As Shawn continued his comments, speaking ponderously now, as if gauging his remarks, Julie felt her imaginings were confirmed.

"Dr. Galbinki is one of those more modern doctors who seem quite comfortable with the idea of cremation. He sees the advantages I mentioned to you, and I know he's recommended our vault cremations to several family members of his patients. Of course, not all agree; some are quite offended. I recall one fairly recent occasion: I heard the doctor . . . hmm, I'd have to say almost arguing with a young woman who was handling her

deceased grandmother's affairs, that she should really opt for vault cremation rather than a fancy burial. His reasons seemed logical; he apparently
knew that she was the only relative who even lived in Florida, and she was
several hours away, so why spend so much of the estate on a fancy mauso-
leum, especially if that wasn't even specified in her will?

"However, I did wonder at the time how the doctor would even know
that; it shows you how close some of these physicians are to their elderly
patients. But anyway, this young woman was quite insistent that money
was no object. She told Dr. Galbinki she was arranging the burial up north
as she knew her grandmother wished, and she didn't want Dr. Galbinki interfering. So of course, he said he understood and didn't pursue it further. I
did feel . . . hmm, let's just say that I would have abandoned the cremation
angle earlier in the discussion. I mean, what difference would it make to
the doctor after all? I suppose he was just trying to protect her pocketbook
a little, do her a favor," Shawn trailed off.

As the assistant director observed Julie and Mike's close attention, he
continued after a moment. "Perhaps Dr. Galbinki assumes special relationships with his patients that make him feel almost like family, but some
survivors may think he takes too much on himself. Just a month or so ago,
there was a similar case, involving a surviving daughter—no young lady,
this one: a very well-spoken and assertive woman, a New York accountant,
I believe—who clearly thought the doctor had overstepped his bounds in
this way. Her mother had died at home, and Dr. Galbinki had certified the
death and had sent her body here. That part was fine. They had arranged to
meet here when she arrived from New York, and that's when we got an earful; you know how these things can happen. The director was out, so I led
her and Dr. Galbinki to a cubicle to wait for him, and well, apparently the
doctor filled the time by suggesting some options, leading with his choice:
the vault cremation. I remember him saying it would be far less expensive
than an ordinary burial and the daughter would still have a site that she
could visit. Well, he didn't even finish when she started yelling at him, 'You
were supposed to be so close with my mother, visiting her, and you don't
know she was a WASP'—I never did understand that word," Shawn said

almost apologetically to Julie and Mike. "I think it meant she was a pilot in World War II or something . . . anyway, she continued shouting at the doctor: 'she will be buried in Arlington National Cemetery with the others who served their country. How dare you even suggest cremation? She's going to Arlington, and I'll make sure the director knows that when I see him.'"

"Well, I obviously couldn't let the conversation continue," Shawn said, "so I stepped over to the cubicle and took the woman to my own private office—with walls to the ceiling," he smiled at Julie and Mike, "you know what I mean, and sat with her until the director returned. I assured her that we would help her out with whatever burial arrangements she wanted, and I thanked her for her mother's service to our country. I believe she was mollified. I did have a word with Dr. Galbinki. I know he was just trying to be helpful to a bereaved woman, but you know, it could have gotten quite sticky. We would have been vulnerable to lawsuit if, God forbid, we'd gone ahead with cremation without the survivor's written instructions. That does sometimes happen in less well-regulated funeral homes, but we've never had any but the best reputation in this regard." Julie could practically see Shawn heaving a sigh of relief in relating this tale, and she and Mike exchanged knowing glances about the subject of his story. *Shawn doesn't know the half of it!* Julie thought.

"We appreciate your candor in speaking with us, Shawn, and please be assured that we will keep this conversation confidential," Julie said. "We won't take up any more of your time." Julie and Mike both shook his hand in leaving, and Shawn gave them his card.

"Feel free to call me if there's any other way I can help," he told them. "And this conversation will remain confidential on my end as well."

As soon as they got outside, Julie said to Mike, "So Galbinki saw the many advantages of cremation in disposing of a body . . ." Mike interrupted, "Yes, and disposing of a body of evidence as well."

Chapter Nineteen

Julie looked at her watch and saw that they still had time to swing by Dr. Galbinki's office in Aventura Mall, which wasn't that far away. "Let's get this visit over with and end this awful day," she said. "I don't expect anything to come of it, but at least I'll know I covered the ground."

"Whatever you say, Julie," Mike agreed. "Then it's back to the timeshare for some laps in the pool, a soak in the hot tub, and dinner at one of those outstanding Miami restaurants you're always raving about."

"Right, and tomorrow you drive," Julie replied. "It shouldn't take the whole day. Just to Miami Palms to get Aunt Lottie's furniture out and then back to her landlady to clear out that apartment." As Julie ran through their schedule, Mike scoped out the upscale Aventura Mall—*Galbinki has an eye for a clientele who don't count their pennies*, he observed as Julie circled into the mall parking lot near Galbinki's office to find a space. Spread out on a grass lawn, the building was an undistinguished glass box in which several doctors had their practice. When they entered the lobby, Julie was surprised to see a different receptionist from the one she knew from her earlier visits with Aunt Lottie. A middle-aged matron of the old school, the previous receptionist had always referred to Galbinki gushingly as "Doctor" as if that were his name, and she ran a tight ship, directing the traffic from the waiting room to the various examining rooms and offices of Galbinki's practice with a firm hand. Instead, now sitting at the reception-ist's desk was an eye-catching blond with expensive painted fingernails, wearing a black cashmere sweater set and beige linen slacks. A young clerk, walking back and forth between the computer and a file cabinet, was also a new addition. *I get that,* Julie thought sourly, *how could Blondie damage her nails digging into those grubby files? Well, let's see how she treats our un-expected visit.* She gave Mike a look that she hoped would warn him that already something seemed amiss.

Mike gazed at the ceiling absently, as Julie looked directly at the receptionist, trying to formulate her request to see the doctor without an appointment in a manner that was not antagonistic but would not brook a refusal. All of a sudden, she took Mike's arm and pressed it surreptitiously, then dropped it quickly and slewed her eyes toward the woman behind the desk. She had just noticed, brilliant against the blond's dark sweater, a diamond heart on a thick gold chain that was the duplicate of Aunt Lottie's most treasured piece of jewelry, the one Julie always tried on when she visited, and that was being saved for her eventual wedding.

Julie forced herself to speak calmly to the receptionist. "Hello, my name is Julie Norman. I'm the niece of Mrs. Lottie Freund, who was Dr. Galbinki's patient for many years. She recently died of a heart attack. I want to thank Dr. Galbinki personally for his many years of care for my aunt—I've met him many times before, when I visited down here. She so appreciated everything he did for her and recommended many of her friends to him. I know I don't have an appointment, but could you please tell him I'm here and willing to wait until he finishes with his patient, just to see him for a few minutes." She smiled helpfully at the blond, who looked unsure of what to do but finally said she would find Dr. Galbinki, and if it wasn't disturbing a patient consultation, she would pass on Julie's request.

Julie and Mike took seats in the waiting room, which only held one other patient, and while Mike picked up a magazine, Julie scribbled a line in her small notebook, which she passed to Mike. "The receptionist is wearing the diamond heart that my Aunt Lottie was saving for me to wear at my wedding." Julie continued to sit in the position of someone who would patiently wait, without distraction, as long as it took to see the doctor. When the receptionist returned, she told Julie that the doctor would spare her a few minutes before he took his next patient. He'd have to make it short, as Julie could see his day was not yet finished. After twenty minutes or so, Dr. Galbinki came out to the waiting room, shook Julie's hand, nodded at Mike's introduction as a friend, and asked them to follow him into his office. "I only have a few minutes," he greeted Julie. "May I offer my condolences on your aunt's death? You know she was one of my favorite patients."

"I know that," Julie said in a sincere tone, "and I want to thank you in person for all the care you gave her over the years. I just want to know if there's anything further about why or how she died than is indicated on the death certificate. 'Natural causes' can mean so many things. Can you be more specific?"

"Not really; your aunt had had several bypass heart operations, and lately she was anxious and depressed. That may have contributed to her death."

"I have to disagree with you, Dr. Galbinki. I don't think she was depressed, and your saying that strikes me as somewhat dismissive. As you know 'depression' is a distinct clinical term that is not necessarily related to one's physical condition. Actually, despite the tragedy of losing her only son, Aunt Lottie did not retreat from life like clinically depressed people. She was very involved in various activities like Hadassah, which were socially stimulating, and her mind was still sharp for sure if her killer card games she minutely described to me in our weekly phone calls were any indication."

"This is not something I am prepared to argue about with you, Ms. Norman," Dr. Galbinki stated with polite indifference. "For an elderly person, or one in a medical facility, unless there's a reason for alluding to a specific cause of death—or the deceased is a suspected victim of a homicide, in which case something like 'asphyxia by strangulation' would be checked off on a police form—the ordinary death certificate is just what you read: 'not trauma injury, not poisoning'—both of which could occur accidentally, of course. The medical profession has chosen simply to emphasize that old people just die, if you'll excuse me putting it so bluntly." The doctor sat back as if he'd just said all that was necessary.

"I understand from Nurse Mendelsohn," Julie persisted, "that you did not feel my aunt's symptoms were life threatening on the night you visited her. You said she was breathing and sleeping well, yet she was dead by the next morning. Does that sequence indicate a particular cause of death?"

"Not in the case of someone with heart problems, say, or pneumonia, or even some cancers. The person may even seem to be improving, but death may come at any unlooked-for moment. If you care to read some medical literature on the subject, I can recommend some books for you."

"No, I think I do understand what you're saying. Again, thank you for your care over the years. We'll let you get back to your work." Julie and Mike left the office while Galbinki remained in his chair.

"That's it for the day, Mike," Julie said. "He's some smoothie, isn't he? If it weren't for seeing that diamond heart, I think I would have walked away satisfied that I'd done all I could in Aunt Lottie's case. But that diamond heart is like Linda's mom's will. It's the step too far that's going to bring him down, a clue to foul play. He probably doesn't know that I knew all about her jewelry. I know it was the same one; it had a distinctive diamond drop from the gold frame of the heart, and the coiled gold chain was also unique. Uncle Sol also had it engraved to my aunt. Maybe Galbinki figured he could score a few points by passing it on to his girlfriend. Scratch the engraving off, maybe, or claim it was a piece his father gave to his mother or whatever? I'll think more about it later. Now we're going to relax. We earned it," Julie said. "And Mike," she added, "I'm so grateful you came along with me. New eyes and ears on the ground, isn't that the expression?"

Early the next morning, the rented U-Haul showed up at the time-share entrance punctually as they'd ordered, and Mike drove it back to Miami Palms with Julie feeding him the directions. True to his word, the young security guard had two burly men standing by to accompany them up to Lottie's apartment. They did a careful, efficient job taking down the few large pieces of furniture, television set, bagged clothing, and some other loose items that Julie wanted Charlotte to sort through before they were offered to Gert or donated to the Hadassah thrift shop. Julie bundled up Aunt Lottie's important papers, photographs, and her velvet bags of jewelry from the same dresser drawer where they'd always lain in the old apartment, securing them in a large purse she'd brought along for the purpose. She wrote out a signed instruction for the security guard that the two helpers should return to the ALF apartment after dropping her and Mike off, and take whatever they wanted that remained. Then they would return the prepaid van to the rental agency. Julie told Mr. Jefferson that she would return to the ALF in a day or so to finalize the paperwork and would be sure to show her appreciation for a job well done at that time. Meanwhile, if any problems arose, she wrote down her telephone number at Aunt Lottie's old apartment and the time-share, for the security guard to call them.

While the moving men emptied the van into Lottie's former apartment, Julie phoned Charlotte to say they were back and she should come over when she could to earmark anything she wanted for herself, her family, or her church. The caregiver arrived within the hour in her "old, blue whale" and greeted Julie with a warm embrace and her deepest condolences on her aunt's death. She shook Mike's hand and thanked him for accompanying Julie at this difficult time. Mike made some coffee while Charlotte and Julie caught up on the past months.

"Charlotte," Julie said, "the rent was paid through this month, so don't let Gert hustle you to get your things out before it's convenient. I'm only sending Aunt Lottie's maple card table set with the four chairs up to New York for myself. Not that I really have space for them, but to me, that's Aunt Lottie, the cutthroat mah-jongg and card player in happier days. The pieces are actually a 1940s set she bought when she got married; it's part of a social life I don't think exists anymore outside of retirement communities down here. Anything else, including all the ethnic art Mom and I brought her back from our travels, is yours or your kids, whatever."

As Mike brought in the coffee and sat down with Charlotte and Julie at the kitchen table, Charlotte told Julie she wanted to share some things of a disturbing nature with her. She hesitated as she looked at Mike.

"Please say whatever you want, Charlotte," Julie urged her. "I've been filling Mike in on all my concerns and the backstory on the whole cast of characters. He's been totally helpful. I will tell you what Aunt Lottie didn't even know: he's a detective in New York, and we're serious about each other. I feel terrible that she'll never get to loop that diamond heart around my neck."

"All right, then," Charlotte said, "and since you mentioned the diamond heart, I'll begin with that. You know how Galbinki ingratiated himself with some of his oldest patients—I don't only mean in age but in years of knowing them, too: Lillian, Lou's mother, and Betty, the one with the rich son who never came down to see her; well, I don't have to list them all. Galbinki would 'stop by' to see them in their homes, fill a prescription for them and bring it over, and just 'drop in' for a cup of tea as he was passing by. You also know that a couple of the women in this building over the years that were under his care in one way or another died—I won't say mysteriously but unexpectedly, when they weren't supposed to be that ill. Of course, they were all old; most didn't have family down here, so Dr. Galbinki handled their death certificates and worked with Comfort Providers Funeral Home to cremate them without actually consulting their relatives. I think most of their families thought he was doing them a favor, but one or two weren't so happy about that. It was a little late in some cases, but if they couldn't be reached right away and the will didn't specify any kind of burial, it was a done deal before they could get themselves together and was certainly the least expensive way to go. It didn't seem like Dr. Galbinki could be lining his own pockets, although I happen to know that quite a few of the residents did leave him 'a little something' in their wills.

"But put that aside for now. You remember Sylvia Stein; she was one of your aunt's favorite canasta partners. She dressed very well, had lots of fancy jewelry, and was quite well off but not snobby, your aunt used to say. Anyway, sometimes Sylvia would hire me for driving errands or call my son to do work around the apartment for her. We knew her grand-daughter, Abby, her closest relative, who lived up in Gainesville and who was also the executor of her estate. Well, some time ago Sylvia died. When Abby came down to clean out her apartment, she hired me and my son to help. All of a sudden she comes running out of the bedroom, shouting, 'Charlotte, where's Grandma's jewelry? Those two pouches she kept in her dresser drawer for me and my sister—they're almost empty.'

"Well, how do I know where they are?" Charlotte turned to Mike and Julie. "I'm thinking, 'little girl, don't accuse me.' That's what happens a lot, you know. You work for someone for years, but if they're missing even a costume bracelet not worth $40, the caregiver or cleaning woman is the first one they blame. In this case, though, Abby squinched her eyes and then said to me, 'Charlotte, what do you know about this Dr. Galbinki? Just the day before she died, Grandma told me he was dropping by for a cup of tea with her. I know she appreciated his many kindnesses, how attentive he was, but what doctor makes house calls these days? I never met the guy; I suppose that's my fault. I had great confidence in all her caregivers, and she never had an emergency I had to run down for, so the occasion just never arose.'

"And then Abby drops the bombshell on me," Charlotte continued. "This little chit of a girl says, 'Charlotte, the next day, the very next day he was supposed to visit Grandma, he calls me to tell me that she died, right in her chair, before he could see her—that's his story. He says that he'd phoned her several times to confirm when he was dropping over, but she never answered her phone. So he drove there and got Gert to open her door, and there she was, "peacefully at rest"—his words. He thought she'd had a stroke; the TV was still on.

"'But you know what I think,' Abby emphasizes to me, 'I think he entered Grandma's apartment, found her comatose in a stroke, and took the opportunity to rifle her drawers. He knew she had expensive jewelry; it was worth a lot of money. In fact, Charlotte, I think he may have killed her for that jewelry, some way that no one would discover. Then he got Gert and pulled the wool over her eyes with his little tale.'" Charlotte blew out her breath. "It's hard to believe, but maybe that little girl's not so dumb.

"And here's why I'm telling you this, Julie: because one day your aunt told me that Dr. Galbinki visited her in her apartment in the ALF—'for a cup of tea,'" Charlotte quoted Lottie but added sarcasm to her voice. "Okay, that was nice of him, I thought. I knew your aunt had taken the apartment with that little kitchen just so she could enjoy a private cup of tea with me, or you when you were visiting, or some special friend she might make at the ALF. So—I don't like to cast suspicions—but I bet that he found a way to see her jewelry; maybe she even showed him the diamond heart she was saving for you. I'd like you to do something for me, Julie. Could you open that pouch now and see if anything's missing?"

"No," said Julie, "I don't have to."

Despite Charlotte's own suspicions of Galbinki, Julie's tale of Aunt Lottie's diamond heart decorating the sweater of the new "receptionist"—she put the word in air quotes—truly shocked her. "The brazenness of him," Charlotte shook her head in disbelief. "Is there a chance Julie can confront him and get back the heart?" she asked Mike.

"Unlikely at this point," he replied. "It's her word against his if there's no engraving on it. But I'm beginning to think that jewelry theft and will forging is just the tip of the iceberg with this guy. Let's keep what we know under our hats for the time being, okay?"

Julie gave Charlotte a bundle of tags and told her to start selecting the items that she might want and asked her to look out for the two guys returning the U-Haul and supervise their moving of the furniture into the apartment. "Just have them put the things anywhere it's convenient," Julie said, "and when it's all done right, thank them and give them this envelope. They know the rental agency where to return the van. Meanwhile, I want to take Mike over to Gert's with me to finish things up there. I'll remind her that it's technically still my apartment. I don't want her coming in with her own key and taking things out until you're finished."

As Julie and Mike crossed the parking lot to the landlady's apartment, Julie noted a gleaming, red hardtop convertible Mercedes parked in one of the resident spaces. *Who in this building drives something like that?* Julie wondered idly. *It must be someone's visiting son.* All the oldsters who still drove stuck mostly to nondescript Toyotas. Unlike the first wave of glossy Cubans who'd immigrated to Miami, the Hispanics who'd begun "taking over" the building, in the favorite phrase of the original tenants, were mostly low-end wage workers driving secondhand pickups or family four-doors showing a lot of wear. When Julie glanced at its license plate, expecting to see the Z denoting a rental, she was taken aback to read LUCKYLOU. *The vanity plate of a gambler who's done all right if he can afford a car like this.* Julie certainly intended to see Lou. He'd left her and her mom a condolence message as soon as he knew about Aunt Lottie's death, and they'd both had short phone conversations with him. Despite the break in the friendship between him and Aunt Lottie in the past year, he *had* been Sol's best friend and helpful to Aunt Lottie as a new widow, and Julie certainly wanted to personally thank him for all his kindnesses.

Catching Gert in her office, and accepting her condolences on her aunt's death, Julie sat down facing her at her desk while Mike stood behind her and smiled vacantly as he was introduced. Julie went down her list of items regarding the apartment and said she would turn in her keys at the end of the month. She told Gert that, at that time, she could take anything left in the apartment. Gert seemed satisfied with the arrangement and told Julie a little bit more about her plans for turning the complex into a retirement facility of some kind. Julie wished her luck and stood up to leave but then mentioned to Gert the beautiful new car Lou was driving these days. "Of course, I'd like to see him while I'm here today; do you know if he's still around since his car is here?"

"Oh, you've missed him, Julie. He doesn't always take his car. He's got some new crony, another gentleman of his age, quite well dressed and not bad looking at all, if you don't count that his one leg drags. But I guess it doesn't affect his driving none. He's got some snazzy ride, too.

Sometimes they take that and off they go. Jai Alai, the Indian casinos, the greyhounds—Lou's pretty lucky I gather. Sometimes, I ask him to place a few bets for me, and I've never come out on the short end yet. His friend's pretty close mouthed, down mouthed, too, not like Lou, who still always has a cheery word for old Gert. Well, I wish you luck with your arrangements down here, and again, I was really sorry to hear about your aunt, especially since she seemed to be liking the new ALF." *You mean the new ALF that killed her,* Julie thought, but what she said was "Thank you, Gert."

Chapter Twenty

The next morning, finishing breakfast on their terrace at the time-share, Mike told Julie, "One more piece of business: I want to call Ernesto and set up lunch. He works out of Miami-Dade headquarters. Does that work for us today?"

"Absolutely, Mike. Set it up. See if he can meet us at the Versailles. He'll know it. I'm salivating over their ceviche and flan already. I'll clear; you call." As she walked in through the living room with the dishes, she heard Mike greeting his buddy. "Sounds perfect, amigo," Mike said, and then he motioned her to the phone. "Hang on a sec, Ernesto. Give Julie the directions; she apparently knows the place."

"Ernesto, I'm so looking forward to meeting you," Julie began, "but forget the directions. I know the way to the Versailles blindfolded. If you get there before us, I want two ceviches, and I'll pick out my two flans when I get there." Julie chuckled in response to whatever the detective had said and put down the receiver. "Two o'clock, Mike," she told him. "He guaranteed 'we'll fatten up that skinny Sicilian.'"

When Julie and Mike arrived at the Versailles, the hub of little Havana, at 2:00 p.m., the restaurant, the size of an airplane hangar, still had a good crowd. But there was no line outside as there always was for the regular lunch and dinner hour, which attracted not only local families but also

politicians and business and media people. The portions were huge and delicious and the prices so reasonable it was hard to believe, Julie told Mike.

Mike spotted his friend right away, standing at the doorway, kibitzing
with the restaurant owner's son who acted as maitre d'. Ernesto was a
beefy guy in a white guayabera hanging over dark pants. Julie observed
that he had a pleasant, fair-skinned, somewhat pockmarked face, expres-
sive dark brown eyes, thick black hair, and a thick moustache. The Cuban
detective grabbed Mike in an affectionate embrace. "Really good to see
you, *amigo*. And this must be the smart, kind, and beautiful Julie," he
shook her hand, obviously admiring Julie in her seersucker "playsuit."
"Don't be modest," he added. "This guy gives me an earful every time we
talk, and I know it's all true 'cause he's a cop and cops don't lie. And I
can see it with my own eyes."

"You can see smart and kind with your own eyes?" Julie joked. "That's a
talent I'd like to have; is it something they put in the drinking water down
here?"

After the busboy set out water and bread on their table, and a passing
waiter laid down three enormous red-covered menus, Ernesto drew out
a book from his black shoulder bag and passed it over to Mike and Julie.
"Here's something you guys should read. I got a copy off Amazon. The
cases aren't all that recent, but what it has to say is, unfortunately, still very
relevant down here on the Gold Coast. It's written by a detective named
Joe Roubicek, who was working out of Fort Lauderdale on a special elder
abuse squad. He brought down some really bad people with his criminal
investigations, but he did even more than that. He was an elder advocate
and a spokesman for better laws regarding the elderly. The book tells
about abusive, criminal, and even violent elder abusers—caregivers, some
doctors and nurses, and a few religious leaders, too. You can't believe the
cons and swindles these people put over on our old folks. It's layman's
language, Julie," he emphasized. "You're both gonna learn a lot from it, I
guarantee. Of course, all these investigations take years; people think it's
like *CSI*, case solved in an hour through this Grissom guy and his little
band of merry men—and gals—and their scientific skills and high-tech

equipment. They don't give much respect to the *humint*—that's a military term for human intelligence, Julie, what we call CIs, 'confidential informants,' not somebody you'd want your daughter to marry, but you're not gonna find a padre in a crack house, right? Also different from *CSI*, a lot of Roubicek's bad guys got away with it, scientific evidence or not. You ever watch that show?" he asked Julie. "Lotta wishful thinking. If only we convicted as many bad guys as they do—you notice they never show the trials where a pricy defense lawyer makes sure the evildoer walks. Perfect justice? Only on TV.

"Anyway, to get back to the present. Naturally, the Gold Coast is the prime stomping ground for medical piranhas. Fact is, old people are the Gold Coast's gold, you better believe it. Agriculture's rocky with all this climate change, the military bases are closing down, one oil spill'll clear the beaches faster than you can say Jackie Robinson, and if you thought real estate was the answer, I got a bridge I can sell you. People can't sell their houses, but they can't refinance them either. And the few jobs that are available pay crap; even our public service sector, teachers, cops, like that, are about the worst paid in the country. But you know who's still got a few bucks worth stealing? The old folks, who played by the rules, saved their scratch, and are just trying to live out their lives in a relatively modest way in good weather. State and city officials down here have become a lot more sensitive about treating senior issues seriously, more public transportation, more designated police squads on elder abuse . . . senior citizens are the most solvent citizens we got.

"Okay, lemme get off my podium now," Ernesto said as the waiter approached to take their orders. "I told Manny, the owner's son I was talking to outside, that we were going to be here for a while, doing business. So we bought the table for the duration; don't worry about it." Julie didn't even open her menu. "A double order of the ceviche appetizer and a side order of *maduras* for me," she told the waiter. Ernesto pointed out some Cuban specials to Mike, who ordered the pork chops *cubano* with "whatever comes with it," and Ernesto stuck to shrimp in garlic sauce. "Less fattening," he said to Julie and Mike almost apologetically. "You know the cop thing: we get less exercise than bus drivers, especially down here in car heaven, and we scarf up the calories like we're *campesinos*. That's why our Cuban guayaberas are worn *outside* our pants. I don't know how this guy keeps in such good shape," he slapped Mike on the shoulder. "Course, I got ten years on him," he said to Julie. "So, how's the trip been; having fun?"

"You bet, Ernesto," Julie replied. "I'm going to get Mike to do Zumba tomorrow; have you ever tried that? Guaranteed to work the pounds off pronto."

"Yeah, I tried it from the couch. My wife made me watch it on TV once," Ernesto replied. "I saw five minutes of it and told her 'what, you want me to die of a heart attack so you can take my job?'"

Julie laughed. "We're also planning a trip to Overtown and one to the Everglades. Do you do a lot of outdoor Florida stuff down here? There's a lot more to Florida than people think."

"Nah, it's not really my thing. Yeah, once, when my brother came down from Jersey with his kids, we went to some ecological talk given by a park ranger, real Smokey the Bear with deceased marine specimens from Biscayne Bay. He passed them around to the bunch of us standing in a circle—my sister-in-law was smart enough to take a nap—but there was me, my brother, his teenage daughter, and son, a nice kid; he's twelve. Well, anyway, Ranger Rick or whoever passes around a huge empty turtle shell. Fine, my niece thinks this guy is cute so she's going, 'oh awesome.' Then a spiny sea urchin was passed around; she pretended great interest, you know, handling all this stuff, and then he takes out a sea cucumber." He paused and was surprised to see Julie biting her lips to hold back a guffaw. "Well, maybe Julie knows what it looks like," he winked at her, "but Mike, this sea thing, it *does* look like a cuke, but sort of slimy like one ya forgot in the fridge for a week. To me, I'm thinking, it looks like—excuse me, Julie—a limp penis but with tiny little eyes and a pinhole of a mouth at the thinner end. So Mr. Jerk that I am, I'm standing closest to the ranger so he lays it on my hand, and the kids are scrunching up their faces and going 'eeweew, gross,' and the adults got these sick smiles on their faces. So then this gray-haired lady, maybe a senior, but a sixties hippie type, know what

I mean?"—"Yeah, yeah," Mike smirked, his shoulders already heaving with suppressed laughter, "probably Julie's mom"—"Wait, wait, I'm not finished," Ernesto protested. "She takes it from my hand, holds it up for a sec, and then says in this loud teacher voice, 'Ranger Rick, did you know the Chinese consider these a great delicacy? They eat them with black bean sauce.' I thought everyone was gonna barf right there."

"Definitely Julie's mom," Mike spit out through his guffaws, and even Julie laughed. "Culture counts, with food as in all things," Julie said with mock severity as the waiter placed their food on the table. "So please excuse me while I tuck right into my raw fish."

As they dug into their huge portions and hunks of the fresh-baked Cuban bread, Ernesto entertained Julie with the tale of how he met Mike. "Julie, you'da loved this crime scene. Some old Cuban doctor, way past his prime, but he 'volunteered' in some clinic in a poor neighborhood. They don't check too close; he didn't turn up for work one day, so they call head-quarters, the senior squad. A bunch of us roll over to his house right away. We see him dead on the floor of the living room. Okay, but you gotta see this—maybe Mike told you—I showed him the photos. This house looks like a Santeria shrine: every bit of floor space is filled, the walls, the tables covered with flowers, altars with botanical candles, ribbons, devil masks, flowers in vases, you name it. The Cuban version, maybe you know Julie; there's a Cuban Santeria, a Haitian Santeria, Brazilian . . . this place is so weird one of the uniforms steps inside, turns right around and says 'Sarge, I can't go in there; I'm a Catholic' . . . and runs out."

"Politically incorrect," Julie only half smiled. "I hope you docked his pay."

"Nah, we gave him some babysitting job on the lawn," Ernesto answered, watching her face closely. "Well, anyway, this doc is a senior; he's sure been abused. We take the investigation. But what's the senior link? We can't find it. So then it turns out this guy is gay; some local kid had been harassing him and his boyfriend; and the hate crimes unit gets into it. They interview the kid. He's got a rock solid alibi; he wasn't even in town then. The boyfriend? A domestic? Nope, not that either. So we're U-turning all over the place, and nothing pans out. Finally, it turns out later, what happened was, this guy had left his keys in his white caddy outside the house, and some doped-up petty thief wanders by, sees the car, takes a look, uses one of the keys to enter the house, kills this guy for his pocket money, steals the car, and drives it up to New York. Of course, the car's on our watch list; some wide-awake uniform up in Queens eyeballs the Florida plates, checks it out, and the idiot is up against the hood in a split second. Now they got him good, but they need some *mature, reliable* detective to go *mano a mano* with him down to Miami. But Mike was the only one free"— this time Julie smirked, "Gotcha!"—"and that was the start of a beautiful friendship," Ernesto concluded.

"Great story," said Julie, picking up the table's three-page foldout dessert folder with fifteen choices of flan, all described and pictured in brilliant colors. "Coconut flan I know, for sure, but for the second one I'll have—how about this Mike—I could let you have a little taste: 'New York cheesecake flan.'"

"I'll skip," said Ernesto. "Coffee all around, and now we'll talk business."

"I really appreciate your spending time on this," Julie said earnestly. "Mike filled you in on the two deaths we're concerned with, my aunt's and her friend Lillian's. You know about the forged will from her daughter Linda, who came to see you, right? And she told you why she was suspicious that her mom might have been murdered?"

"Yeah," agreed Ernesto, "she told us the whole story. She's a sharp lady, had all her numbers in place. We started up an investigation, first to prove the forgery of the will, and now we go on foot, door to door, build a case for the murder if we get the evidence, and maybe find an eyewitness. We'll keep Linda up to date on it and keep Mike and you in the picture, too. So now tell me about your aunt. Mike said you suspect wrongdoing in her death but more on the basis of the cast of characters than on any forensic evidence; is that right? I don't have any pieces of the puzzle except this doctor, Galbinki. We ran the databases like Mike did and got about the same information. No convictions, no trials even, but it definitely makes him a person of interest. And he's your aunt's doctor, too. That's it so far, right?"

"No, now there's something new," Julie emphasized. "Mike and I visited Esther Mendelsohn, the night nurse in the nursing home facility of the ALF where Aunt Lottie was living. My aunt was there for some suspected blood clot and heart palpitations; Dr. Galbinki was going to run some tests if she didn't improve. He's the 'on call' doctor at this facility and saw her the night she died. According to a Nurse Mendelsohn, she saw Dr. Galbinki there; he'd been in to see my aunt, of course. This was about 10 p.m. He said he left her sleeping well and didn't want her disturbed. He cautioned the nurse not to go into the room, just peek from the doorway, and let my aunt sleep. She's another of Galbinki's fans and did exactly what he told her. So if my aunt was really sleeping and died naturally later on, or was killed by Galbinki and the nurse just *assumed she was asleep*, we don't know. Then, when we visited Galbinki's office, I saw that his new, eye-candy receptionist was wearing what I know is my aunt's diamond heart necklace. We couldn't look for the inscription, of course, but maybe, even it was removed, later on some traces could be restored to prove Galbinki stole it."

"That's burglary, not homicide," Ernest replied kindly, "but Mike probably told you that already. And a good defense lawyer could even claim that your aunt *gave* him the heart to give to 'a loved one.'"

"No way," Julie asserted with certainty, "not this particular necklace." She then explained to Ernesto how her aunt had promised it to her for her wedding. "And there's another new thing we know," Julie continued, repeating Charlotte's story verbatim about the missing jewelry from a neighbor, discovered by her granddaughter after her death. "Abby told Charlotte right then and there that she thought her grandmother had died in suspicious circumstances. It seems that the old lady had mentioned looking forward to a visit from Dr. Galbinki, who'd been her regular doctor for many years. Abby told Charlotte that he was going to bring her grandma new medication for some minor illness that hadn't responded to treatment.

Abby hadn't met Galbinki but was very cynical about her grandma's belief in his devotion to his patients. 'Imagine,' her grandma had told Abby, 'who else but dear Dr. Galbinki would spend a few minutes of his own Sunday to sit and chat over a cup of tea with an old lady—he's so kind.'"

Julie then repeated Shawn's story from the funeral home, without mentioning the details of his confidential conversation. "He never mentioned Abby's name, but after hearing Charlotte's story, we knew he must be referring to her," Julie asserted, while Mike nodded agreement and took up the story.

"Even Shawn wondered aloud to us why the physician of the deceased would argue so strenuously for a cremation in light of a close family member's contrary wishes," Mike said. "Do the relatives a favor to their pocketbook, fine; he could understand that. But go any further—what purpose could that serve?"

"Well, guys," Ernesto said, addressing them both, "here's something we've just begun to rethink in building our case against Galbinki. Like I said, right now he's just a 'person of interest' with Linda's mom, maybe later on with your aunt and this old lady Charlotte told you about. When we reviewed certain hospital records, North Miami General, for instance, where Galbinki had visiting privileges, we did find several other registered complaints about unexpected, suspicious deaths. Some of these *were* Galbinki's patients, and with his suspect medical resume we thought a useful pattern was developing. But Galbinki had strong alibis for some of these deaths, and the victims didn't exactly fit the profile. One that happened in January was a middle-aged man and then, a couple of months later, a young male car accident victim who was in a coma and on life support. We shuffled those off to Homicide, and they're doing their own investigations. We're keeping each other in the loop. It's beginning to appear that there are two parallel tracks here that may have nothing to do with each other. It's not gonna be cleared up any time soon; I can tell you that. Prosecutors don't *have to* show motive to charge a suspect if the evidence is strong, but any DA's office is gonna be awful shy about putting some well-respected physician on trial without a motive. And we just don't see yet what Galbinki gains from the deaths of the women who died: a few pieces of jewelry, even good jewelry. Not too convincing for a guy with a successful practice like he has."

As Ernesto wound down, Julie surreptitiously took the check that the waiter had laid on the table and excused herself. When she returned, she saw Ernesto looking around for the bill. She confessed with a tiny smile. "I got it, Ernesto. Don't even protest; it's coming out of a grant I received to do my fieldwork down here. You're one of my informants . . . I mean collaborators." Julie shook her head in mock despair. "We've got to find another term for the folks who help us in our work," she said, "but whatever, it's on me."

"Isabella's gonna kill me, Julie. Anyway, we plan to have you over for a *home-cooked* Cuban family dinner, my *abuelito*, the kids, the whole ball of wax—no shop talk, just relaxing in the back yard. So let's set a date."

"You bet," said Julie, "that's what we anthropologists call 'reciprocity.'"

Chapter Twenty-One

"KIA: Killer in Action," Mike crowed to Julie as he swung into the driver's seat of their little Korean rental. Although Julie had been doing most of the driving so far, she decided Mike could handle the I-95 to Boca better than she. He hadn't stopped smart-mouthing the Florida drivers since they'd arrived, though he knew better than to backseat drive *her*.

"You know you're in Florida when the cars are driven by headless people," he complained. "Damned old duffers gripping the wheel at ten and two like they were taught sixty years ago," he groused to Julie as she gave him directions from the map opened on her lap. She smiled at his frustration and opened her window to take in the fresh, early morning Florida air.

Julie hoped that her old friend Rhoda, an attractive woman in her fifties who'd been living in Florida for several years, would be able to clue her and Mike into the medical scene on the Gold Coast with some information that might relate to her Aunt Lottie's death. Rhoda had taken early retirement from her supervisory job at New York's Board of Education and, for a while, had continued to live with her widowed dad in their comfortable brownstone in Brooklyn. He was a fit and feisty retired construction worker who now lived in Delray Beach, not far from Rhoda. From her occasional letters and phone calls, Julie knew that her friend had met a man at her condo development—"Please, Julie, don't call it a development,"

Rhoda had told her. "That's for places like where Dad lives. Barry'll explain the whole retirement and Medicare scene from A to Z," she'd assured Julie. "I bet he'll be able to help you."

In little over an hour, Mike turned off I-95 for Boca Raton, where Rhoda lived in a gated community, and followed the directions to its guardhouse. While the guard checked Julie's name on his clipboard list, Mike turned his fist into a gun, directing Julie's attention to his sidearm. *Big debates over that in the security industry,* Julie recalled. Rhoda had been embarrassed when she had mentioned it by saying that her upscale community had had a lot of burglaries, and it was just a safety thing. *And maybe a class thing, too,* Julie thought. Mike carefully followed the guard's surprisingly complicated directions to Rhoda's house, winding slowly around the cunningly designed hairpin curves bordering a fake lake. *Are there any real lakes on the Gold Coast?* Julie wondered. They passed a Day-Glo-green golf course and extensively planted streets from behind which peeked some mansion-sized homes. Julie was mildly surprised that her prim and proper friend would have gone for the big bucks and fancy living the place implied, but Julie knew she'd get a lengthy and candid answer from Rhoda as soon as they sat down.

After covering practically the whole community, Mike pulled to a halt in front of a cozy little detached house whose front door bore the brass numeral they were searching for. The red, lavender, and pink papery leaves of brilliant bougainvillea vines framed the doorway, and glorious hibiscus bushes bordered the small front lawn. Rhoda was waiting in front, very Florida in a pastel alligator-logo polo shirt and matching Bermuda shorts. She kissed Julia enthusiastically on both cheeks and shook Mike's hand. "Your property's just beautiful," Julie said. "I didn't expect anything so grand."

"Oh, there's a story about how I could afford this place," Rhoda said right away, ushering them into the house. "Barry, the entertainment director at the place where I lived with my dad when we first came down here, found it for me. It was much cheaper than it should have been because it backs onto the local high school—you'll see that when we go out on the patio. There's a covered chain-link fence between the properties, of course, but still, a lot of retirees don't fancy a bunch of high school kids making out and smoking joints so close to their home. The doctor who bought it—his stocks tanked, and he couldn't afford to keep up the mortgage, so he was willing to take a bath on the sale. Barry took me to a place where I could buy all consignment furniture, and since I wasn't going to pay the seventeen thou for the golf privileges, I really could manage it. Barry said I paid my dues in the city schools for so long, why shouldn't I enjoy my retirement in style?"

Rhoda took Julie's hand and drew her into the free-flow living and dining area that made the place look larger than it was. Seated on a white sectional couch watching a mammoth flat-screen television was a large man with a boyish chubby face and a fashionably razor-cut head of salt and pepper hair. He turned casually toward Rhoda and her friend. "And this is Barry," Rhoda introduced him, "and, Barry, this is my friend Julie; I've told you about her. And her friend Mike."

Barry didn't rise, but he half turned over the back of the couch to greet them, keeping his eyes on the baseball game that filled the TV. "How're you doing, guys?" he asked. "I hope you don't mind me not being sociable right now, but I just wanna see the Red Sox put the Yankees out of their misery. Mike, you wanna join me? The girls probably have a lot to talk about anyway, and the game's nearly over." *Girls*, Mike hooted to himself as he nodded to Barry and took a seat on the couch. *Julie could axe him for that.*

"Yes, we do," Rhoda replied without chiding Barry. "You two join us outside when the game's over." The two women walked out to the patio, which faced a small swimming pool. "It's really just for dunking, not swimming," Rhoda admitted, "but the clubhouse has a real lap pool, not that hardly anyone uses it." Before settling into the pillowed wrought-iron chairs grouped around a square, glass-topped table, Julie wandered over to the wrought-iron trellis upon which climbed a number of exquisitely delicate white- and pastel-colored flowers. "Oh, my goodness, are these orchids?" Julie asked her friend. "Yes they are," answered Rhoda proudly. "I shouldn't admit it, but they're quite easy to grow."

"So tell me Rhoda," Julie began as they took their chairs. "How did all this come about? This gorgeous place you have? Don't leave out a thing."

"It is a bit of a story," Rhoda replied in the careful way Julie was accustomed to in their friendship. "You know, I thought I was doing the right thing, staying in that big, old house in Carroll Gardens after Mother died, sticking close to Dad when he retired. But then one day he just upped and announced that he was going down to pinochle heaven, in South Florida, to be near an old construction buddy who'd taken a place down there. He was ready for some of the warms, as he said. After all the years working high up on those slippery scaffolds in all kinds of weather, who could blame him? He wasn't going to sell the house, he insisted. He had enough from his pension, Social Security, and his savings to cover his new life down there and then some. But when I took my early retirement, I thought I should move down there, too, to be near him, I mean. He was healthy then, but that couldn't last forever, and I wanted to be closer than a plane ride away." *Aha*, Julie clicked on the connection, *that's where Rhoda got the extra few bucks for this beautiful deal. And more than a few bucks. Her family's Carroll Gardens house cost next to nothing when they bought it; the nabe was full of blue-collar working Italians like themselves, not yuppified like it became later.*

"So, first," Rhoda continued her tale, "he got a rental in Sunrise Village, all the way out on Sunrise Highway. It was so far from the ocean you'd think you were in Kansas. The place had some amenities, but my dad and I in that poky two bedroom . . . it didn't really work. Most days Dad carpooled with the other guys who were bored there out in the boonies and worked a part-time job at the nearest Home Depot. In the evenings, they played cards or shot pool in the clubhouse or watched some action film they'd show there.

"Some of the folks there were the 'young old,' you know, recent retirees in their sixties and seventies. I guess you could say Dad and his buddies were the 'old,' in their early eighties, but they get around fine, slowing down a bit physically but still have all their marbles. But most of the folks there were the 'old old,' the frail elderly, mostly with caregivers or—you'll love this, Julie—with girlfriends. Yes, in their eighties and nineties even, hooking up with each other, don't ask me what they do, but you'd see them around the pool or standing in the water, kibitzing, whatever. Barry was the entertainment director and golf pro; there was a small course, but neither Dad nor I play golf, and there was no one my age. Depressing. And the maintenance was terrible, too. Does Mike like alligators? He'd love this. One day I open the front door for my morning walk, and there's an alligator on my doorstep. All right, just a baby but still! And the bathtub Jacuzzi they promoted . . . when I turned it on, huge water bugs came crawling out of the drain. I never used the darn thing!

"Actually, it was Barry who suggested I move. He was leaving his job there anyway, and he heard about Boca Lakes. He also knew of a really nice gated community nearby that had an ALF on the premises, but the whole place is more like a regular neighborhood, not just retirees. Dad can't stand to think of himself living just with old people. It was win-win for both of us. He has real streets to walk on, a mall nearby, a library, and even some public transportation. There are more New Yorkers there, his kind of people. He even has a girlfriend. He'd love to see you, and then you'll hear all about the retirement alternatives down here. He's really enjoying himself, even though he won't admit it."

At that point, Mike and Barry came out of the living room. Mike took a seat, while Barry stood with his hands in his perfectly pressed pants pockets and took their drink orders. "Just seltzer or water, Julie, and Coke for you, Rhoda?" he asked. "You're not putting my talents to work here."

When Barry returned with the drinks, Rhoda started to explain Julie's concerns. "Barry, Julie is interested in the ALF situation down here. Her aunt was in Miami Palms"—"Miami Palms?" Barry interrupted. "I know that place, down in Little Haiti. Now, why'd your aunt want to stay there with all those drug dealers? There're so many nicer places up this way;

they're going for *bupkes* now the economy's in the toilet. I have a few bucks invested in the industry; I could have told you the score."

"Barry," Rhoda admonished him before Julie could correct his assumption that her aunt was still in the market for a place. "Julie's aunt just died in the nursing home facility at Miami Palms. She can't get a straight answer from the management about what exactly happened."

"Oh, jeez, I'm really sorry for your loss, Julie," Barry said. "I shouldn't have butted in. But the fact is I *do* know a lot about the retirement situation here, and I'm happy to help. Fire away."

"I just don't know what questions to ask, Barry; that's part of the problem. And that Dr. Galbinki my aunt swore by . . . Mike and I feel like he's not on the up and up, what he's telling us."

"Oh yeah, Galbinki," Barry explained, "all the LOLs adore him."

"LOLs?" Mike asked. "What's that mean?"

"Little old ladies, my friend. He's very cozy with them. The relatives who haven't seen the deceased in a dog's age—they come out of the woodwork, sniffing around some big lawsuit, malpractice against a doctor, neglect in an ALF or hospital, whatever. Galbinki's the industry's smoothie. Certifies 'natural causes' on the death certificate—that's gold. The medical culture down here, very cagey, one hand washes the other. He gives them cover. I don't say he'd lie, no, but lay people don't get it. They think, 'but you gotta die of something.' No, you don't! No trauma? No poisoning? Over eighty? Can't prove a thing. The relatives slink away without a sou. I've seen it a million times. But if you think the ALF was negligent in some way, I know a lawyer who can sell you a lawsuit that will fit you to a T and give you some practical condolences for your aunt's death."

"Barry," Rhoda chided. "Julie's not down here to collect on some lawsuit. She told me her aunt had heart surgeries before, and Julie," Rhoda turned to her friend, "it *is* possible she died of heart failure just like the doctor said, isn't it?" Julie tilted her head a bit to indicate that could be true.

"And there's something else you might want to check out. There's a black guy named Eric, black as pitch but handsome as a model, even with those long dreads they call 'em, tucked up into some kind of knitted hat; he's a freelance caregiver, knows every medical piece of action on the Gold Coast. He plays chess with the old men and drives the old ladies to the shopping . . . he gets a lot of private paid overtime from the ALFs. He'll tell ya straight up; some of those old folks even left him a hunk of change in their wills. Your dad knows him, right, hon? And he lives real close by."

"Would you like to see my dad?" Rhoda asked Julie. "You were always his favorite friend at our Christmas parties."

"I'd love to see him," Julie answered. "His politics were right up my alley. I bet he won't be shy about telling it like it is."

"You got that right," Barry laughed. "That man is a pistol. Complaints day and night, right, hon?" Julie was taken aback by his intimate tone and Rhoda's acceptance of his description. *Hmm*, Julie figured it out now. Rhoda hadn't asked to make it a foursome. With Barry in the picture she was still close to her dad, but *not that close. Probably wiser to keep them apart*, Julie conceded to herself.

"Let me check that he's home," Rhoda put her cell phone to her ear and arranged the visit in a few minutes. "He's looking forward to seeing you," she said, closing the phone. "It's easy to find; I'll give you the directions. But first, we eat."

As Rhoda went out to the kitchen to start bringing out the food, Barry said sincerely, "What a gal! She's the only one in this whole damn place who doesn't do take-in or eat out three meals a day."

Julie and Mike agreed that Barry had it made, as they drove away after lunch. "Now to see the pistol," Julie laughed, as Mike cocked his fist into a gun for the second time that day.

Chapter Twenty-Two

Following Rhoda's directions, Julie headed to Military Road and turned left, passing a bunch of look-alike retirement communities, walled in by hedges that resembled the perpetual-care trimmed bushes of Long Island cemeteries. *An apt comparison*, Julie thought. Lots of billboards for lawyers, too—she especially liked "lawyerup"—and a sign in front of a bank: "still strong, still lending." That, along with the many folks standing on the roadway with signs proclaiming "cash for gold," confirmed the impact of the economic downturn on the Gold Coast. As she began the turn into Rhoda's father's community, her attention was momentarily distracted by a man standing with a large sign hoisted on a pole on the roadside in front of the entrance to another gated community whose large sign read Winding Creek in elegant italic script. *A very upmarket place*, Julie judged, scanning the entrance fountain and guardhouse. She slowed down a little to check it out. *What is this guy doing there with his sign?* He was wearing camouflage pants, a multipocketed fisherman's vest, a baseball cap whose logo Julie couldn't read, and military-style sunglasses. A bicycle lay on the grass nearby him. His sign read "Dr. Stevens, the Worst Ever" in huge letters, and just below in smaller print, "in my opinion." When he saw Julie giving him the onceover, he twisted the sign around so she could read the other side: "Home/Office of a Cock-a-Hoop Arrogant Crybaby" written in huge, red letters. The 516 area code phone number below these words was presumably that of the doctor.

"I hope this guy'll still be here when we come back," Julie nudged Mike to take a look. "I'd like to interview him. Or maybe Rhoda's dad knows him, sounds like his kind of guy."

They drove into the driveway of Sherwood Forest, where Rhoda's father lived. "Sherwood Forest?" Mike snorted. "Where the hell is a forest around here? Who makes up these names?" Ignoring Mike's sarcasm, Julie stopped at the barrier, while Mike got out and punched the numbers Rhoda had given him into the code box in front of an empty guardhouse. The barrier lifted, and they drove past what looked like a small clubhouse, a fountain spouting water into another man-made lake and a vista of palm trees. *But not royal palms, like at Rhoda's place,* Julie noted. A garbage truck was parked off a communal lawn, and a couple of Hispanic-looking men, presumably maintenance people, were playing a pickup soccer game.

"Hey, Mike," said Julie, as they drove up to Rhoda's father's house and parked outside the one-car garage. "Can you already see American social stratification in action?"

"Huh," queried Mike, "we're not even inside yet, and you're already doing anthropology; what did I miss?"

"It's subtle, Mike, but it's there. Did you notice, no guard at the gate, never mind no gun; the clubhouse is tiny compared to Rhoda's; the fountain is half the size of Boca Lakes—that's a $25,000 difference in the housing price; and the homes we've passed only have one-car garages. I'm going to check with Dom; I bet he'll confirm what I'm saying and be able to add a whole lot more. See why I always carry my trusty notebook . . . and my digital camera, too? I can use the photos as the basis for . . ."

"Your research." Mike interrupted her, laughing but impressed despite himself. "And yeah, I do see it now that you point it out."

Dominic, Rhoda's father, answered their first ring at the front door of a small, two-story house with a welcoming smile. He was a tall, sturdy-looking man with a full head of grey hair, somewhat tousled, who was maybe in his early eighties. He wore chinos and Birkenstock sandals—

"the sure sign of a socialist," Julie's friend Mary used to joke—and a Che Guevara T-shirt. He gave Julie a hearty hug and shook Mike's hand firmly. Behind him stood a petite woman with a grey pixie haircut, wearing a thin Indian kurta, cutoff denim shorts, and ballet slippers.

"Come out to the Florida room," Dom invited them. "Helen will bring out the coffee." He guided Julie and Mike through a spacious room to a small glassed-in patio.

"Why do they call it a Florida room?" Mike asked as they all seated themselves around the rattan-trimmed, frosted glass table. "You're in Florida; aren't all the rooms Florida rooms?"

"You got me. I asked the same question when I got down here," Dom chuckled. "I still don't have the answer." Just beyond the patio's screen doors was a narrow lawn dotted with cabbage palms that Mike mistakenly took for fakes, and a canal on which swans were swimming. In the distance, they saw a golf course where a few elderly men dressed in Bermuda shorts, golf shirts, and baseball hats stood over their tees, while others were riding around the course in open-sided golf carts.

"Do you play golf?" Julie asked Dom politely. Rhoda's dad scowled, while Helen, who'd just entered with the coffee tray and a plate of home-baked cookies, patted his arm gently. "Don't get him started on golf courses," she said calmly to Julie, "or you'll get his lecture on how Florida development, with all the golf courses and sprinklers, is using up the water supply while Africans and South Americans and people in India don't even have clean drinking water."

"You can mock me if you want, Helen, but it's true. There *is* a growing scarcity of water in the world, even right here in the Everglades. So much water is wasted in our tropical resorts like Florida and Hawai'i, just so some old farts can hit a ball with a stick so it falls into a hole. And this isn't *our* golf course, Julie; that's for the upper-uppers, like where Rhoda lives. This place is for hoi polloi. Americans say we have no class system; we're all middle class. What a joke. It's all socially graded here; you just have to look carefully. We have a small community pool and an outdoor Jacuzzi. I have to admit that feels good for the old bones. But our clubhouse only has a small exercise room, no fancy restaurants like at Rhoda's. And we've got sabal palms, not Royal palms. This place is actually pretty down to earth, with mostly retired working people inside the gates—white collar, true, but there's also regular working folks with families, and guys and gals that actually go to jobs and take care of their own lawns, not like in Rhoda's place, where it's all hired landscapers and what have you. Those people don't do anything with their own hands."

"Dom, Dom, stop punishing yourself with your guilt about living in comfort," Helen admonished him. "You worked hard your whole life. What's so terrible if you relax a little in your old age?"

"Yeah, yeah, you're right, honey." Dom sheepishly acknowledged what was obviously an ongoing conversation between them. Then, turning to Julie and Mike, he said, "It *is* the good life, no question. And most of us, even the folks in Rhoda's place, didn't *inherit* their wealth either. A lot of them came from the ranks and worked themselves up in business, law, and medicine, whatever, going to school for a zillion years—the American Dream come true. I'm really all for it; it's just that it's so unequal. Once, I heard the governor of Florida say, 'When capitalism and competition win, everybody wins.' So I wrote him a six-page, single-spaced letter listing the losers and explaining what they lost. He never did write me back."

"Gee, I can't image why," Helen said with a grin. But Dom rolled right on.

"And where are the minorities? Segregation might have gone out officially, but d'you see any black people here? Any Hispanics? No way, they have their own *ungated* communities. There're Haitian people down the road maybe two or three miles from here; do you ever see them? *Forget about it*, maybe waiting at a bus stop—another joke. Florida's version of public transportation is a bus an hour, if you're lucky. The two worlds hardly ever mix. Sometimes you see them at the library; gotta say one thing: the libraries down here are great. They have computers and everything and are open on Sunday. They get the *New York Times*, which is five bucks a pop to buy down here, and the *New York Review of Books* and even *The Nation*. So you do see some multiculti at the library, mostly using the computers—otherwise, not. Go to the Wal-Marts; you'll see some blacks there, and not only as stock clerks. It's just down the road, walking distance. I gotta admit I shop there myself, just so I don't have to climb in the car every time I want a loaf of bread. Imagine an old union guy like me, shopping in Wal-Mart! I would never have believed it. The way they treat their people; it's disgusting. But then, their prices are the lowest, so it's good for working people, too."

"We'll have to stop there on the way home, Mike," Julie said. "I've never been to a Wal-Mart. We can call it part of my fieldwork," she grinned.

"So you're doing fieldwork down here?" Dom asked Julie. "I thought Rhoda said it's something about your aunt's death. What happened?" After briefly explaining her new research project, Julie gave Dom and Helen the short version of their investigation into Aunt Lottie's death. She mentioned her suspicions—the merest speculation, she assured him, but just covering the bases—that maybe someone in the health field—who knows, an aide, a nurse, some administrator at the ALF, or maybe even a doctor—had had some role in it, that it wasn't as "natural" as the death certificate said or the ALF manager claimed it was.

"We've been in touch with a police detective in Fort Lauderdale whose specialty is elder exploitation, and we were amazed at some of the things he told us. It's mostly for money, of course; these older people are very vulnerable to exploitation by people pretending to care about them, or for them, but Aunt Lottie didn't have anything to steal—a small diamond heart, a trinket really, was missing, but no big bucks or property that would motivate a killing."

"Yeah, but maybe no one knew that, Julie," Dom suggested. "Someone might have assumed, wrongly, that there *was* money there. A lot of these people do have stashed cash, CDs lying around, investment papers, big checking accounts, Medicare payments, whatever. A smart guy could make off with something if he knew how to do it."

"Yes, that's what the detective told us, so we know we're not paranoid. Mike will be going back to New York in a couple of weeks, but I can stay down here for a while, and I'd really like to figure out what, if anything, happened. Rhoda's boyfriend, Barry"—here Dom snorted—"gave us a good heads up on the medical situation down here. He seems to know what he's talking about, lawsuits, medical malpractice, and all. It gave us some leads, and he mentioned a guy named Eric—he said you know him—who he thought could be helpful."

"Yeah, Barry would know about that; he's got money in the industry, and he knows all the players," Dom agreed. "And I do know Eric; I'll give you his number before you leave. And listen, it's not all bad. Florida may be a haven for corrupt, maybe even criminal, medical people, but that stuff's pretty rare. Most of our doctors and caregivers, people like Eric, are fine people, even more caring than you'd find up north. They know a lot of the old folks down here are all alone, and they do try harder to be attentive, spend more bedside time with them.

"But still, funny things do sometimes happen in these medical facilities. A good friend of ours, mine and Helen's, who lived in North Miami, had to go to the hospital for a blood clot. They're common with the elderly. It didn't seem too serious; they were watching it. But then the next thing we know, bang, the hospital calls that she's dead. She didn't have any family here, and she gave my name as the contact person; that's why they phoned me. We also got the 'natural causes' explanation. But I don't think she had any money that went astray. Who was that doctor she used, Helen, a real pompous ass in my opinion, but everyone else loved him . . . right? He had a funny name, foreign; I think he was from Albania or some weird place."

"Was it Galbinki, by any chance?" asked Julie. "He was my aunt's doctor."

"Yeah, yeah, that's the guy, a real smooth operator. In fact, I talked with Irv Kruger—he's a terrific doctor at the same hospital, North Miami Gen—about this guy. According to Irv, Galbinki's been in some muddy waters before, and he kind of has a reputation for overmedicating his patients. And he does seem to favor the old widows. Then, somehow, they're just gone."

Julie and Mike shot each other significant glances. "We'll keep on checking," Mike said with determination. "It ain't over 'til the fat lady sings."

Chapter Twenty-Three

As Julie reached out for her third cookie, she thanked Helen for the treat and laughed that, if she kept up this South Florida research, she'd weigh two hundred pounds by the time she returned to the city. "So what brought you to Florida, Helen?" she asked.

"Same old, same old, too damn cold up in Chicago, so my husband and I decided to retire here for the climate. He died a couple of years after we got here, and I just stayed on."

"Oh, I'm sorry to hear that," said Julie. "That must have been very difficult for you."

"No, it was heaven," responded Helen, with a small smile. "He was a real control freak, and I actually looked forward to having some freedom for a change."

So much for my stereotypes of the aged, Julie thought, and changed the subject, diplomatically, she hoped, now addressing both Dom and Helen. "Do you guys know anything about that protester with the sign across the road? I thought maybe if he's still there, I could interview him before we head back to Miami."

"Yeah, I've spoken to him a few times," Dom responded after sipping his coffee. "He's a real character—which is not to say he doesn't have a case. Apparently, some dentist screwed up his treatment and wouldn't give him a refund or something. Refund, lotsa luck; the guy thinks he's at Macy's. A dentist's gonna part with a nickel already in his pocket? He seems nice enough, though, just another guy with a legitimate beef he can't win, is all. You got plenty of crackpots down here, though, right-wingers who are nuts on the health care issues."

"Be fair, Dom," said Helen. "They're not all nutcases. Let's just say some of them are ideologically in a different place than you are."

"Have you been to any of the town hall meetings they had on the medical reform issue?" Julie asked. "We read about it in the New York papers, and I even watched a lot of televised hearings, but it's still pretty confusing."

"You think you're confused, Julie; you should hear the people who go to these Tea Party meetings. It's all ideology with them, the culture wars in a different dress. The haves and the have-mores, as our former president Bush used to say. And some of the 'have-lesses' don't even know enough to vote their own best interests. It's the gospel of wealth all over again, like in the age of the robber barons. Just work hard, and save your money; you don't need government help, like highways for moving your goods or cleaning up after a hurricane. Individual responsibility, go it alone, the old bootstraps—that's the American way. These folks don't have a clue. Some guy at one of these town hall meetings shouted, 'I'm for individual liberty; get the government's hands off my Social Security and Medicare.' It made all the papers.

"I went to one of those town hall meetings, up north of here. What a fiasco. Things got really ugly even before it started. The hall was too small to fit everyone in, and the police had to lock hundreds of people outside. Man, they were so angry they began banging on the windows and doors; it started a real riot. The police tried to restore some order so people could speak, but it got so out of hand the cops finally had to send everyone home. At least no one was hurt like in other places. When some poor guy with his son in a wheelchair got up there, trying to tell how the medical reform bill would help the kid, people actually booed. These *gavones* are so misinformed; they're an embarrassment to themselves. They don't even know what the bill will actually do."

"Hmm," Julie pondered. "I think maybe it's cultural as well as political. An American friend of mine who'd lived in France for many years once told me, 'Americans,' he said, 'hate paying taxes, even if it means they don't get services that they want or need. In Europe and Canada, people are willing to pay very high taxes if that's what it takes to provide those services.' Our medical care system is a good example of that. We're one of the few—maybe the only—industrialized nations whose health care is built on a fee-for-service model. Most European countries and Canada consider health care a government responsibility, and people don't mind paying higher taxes for it. It's no coincidence that these folks protesting what they call socialized medicine took that name Tea Party. The Boston Tea Party was an antitax movement after all."

"Socialized medicine," Dom scoffed. "Don't these protestors know we already have socialized medicine? What else are the VA and Medicare? And no one wants to give those up. But I think you're right about culture. We have this big cultural deal about how innovative America is, all this medical technology: 'who'd do all the research and development if they didn't see a profit in it?' yadda, yadda, yadda. But do people know how much unnecessary medical technologies are used just so hospitals and doctors can collect some government dough? Don't get me wrong; the doctors have some legitimate beefs, especially the GPs. They're not the ones making the big bucks; that's why there are so few medical students who choose to go into family practice, especially compared to Canada or England."

"Well," countered Julie, tentatively, "I don't know this from personal experience, but I do hear in Canada, there's a big wait for treatment. That's a big issue for a lot of folks."

"That's all propaganda," Dom retorted. "It's just not true. But Americans are typically so impatient, they can't wait for anything—maybe that's culture again. It's a medical fact: some things don't need to be treated immediately. People in Canada have a longer life expectancy and lower infant mortality than America. Our medical system is so unequal, who gets in and who's left out; don't people care about that? Equal opportunity is also supposed to be an American cultural value. Maybe you anthropologists can figure it out. I sure can't understand it. Anyway, now it's a done deal," Dom said in a resigned voice. "Let's see how it plays out."

As he fell silent, Julie and Mike prepared to leave, and with hugs and handshakes all around, they were soon on their way. Julie hoped the protestor would still be standing where they left him.

As Mike drove out to the barrier, Julie was delighted to see the protester still standing there twirling his sign. "This is a found ethnographic opportunity," Julie told Mike as they pulled over. "Medical culture is such an important part of South Florida's culture."

"Just don't get too close," he cautioned Julie. "With the gun laws down here, some of these people can be dangerous, just waiting for someone to get in their face."

"I'll be careful," promised Julie as she got out of the car and walked over to the protestor with a big smile on her face. "Hi," she grinned in a friendly way. "I was just visiting a friend across the road and noticed your protest. Do you mind telling me what it's all about?"

Close up, the protestor looked a little older than Julie had first thought. His small beard and potbelly made him look almost harmless. He hesitated for a moment, and then said, "Sure, I'll tell you. See, I had this gum problem, and my dentist recommended this specialist. So I went to see him, and he started on a treatment program: full cash payment up front. The doctors down here all take Medicare, no problem; they know which side their bread is buttered, but a lot of the dentists want total cash on the line. The treatment was making me feel worse, so I called this guy's office and asked his receptionist about a refund, and she said, 'We don't give refunds.' I knew the way she said it this wasn't the first time someone had asked for their money back."

"So why are you protesting here? Is this where his office is?" Julie asked.

"Nah, his office is up a ways, in Boynton Beach; know where that is? Sometimes I go there with my sign, but his lawyer sent me a 'cease and

desist' letter. I'm a Vietnam vet. I don't scare easily, and some lawyer's letter doesn't put the fear of God into me. But I found out where this dentist
lived and decided, if I came to this classy gated community with my signs,
it'd poke him in the eye even better."

"And has it?" asked Julie. "Have any of the residents spoken with you?"

"They sure have," the protester replied. "They're pissed as hell at him.
It's a big embarrassment for them to have me here. And I ain't going away
any time soon, either. Yesterday, I got a couple of illegals to stand with
me. I dig them up at Home Depot, places like that; they're all there looking for extra cash and will do anything for ten bucks an hour. They add a
little more excitement, right? This dentist is going to owe me plenty when
I send him my bill. I'm going to charge him $1000 a day for every day I'm
here—it's been three weeks already—and give it all to the American Cancer Society. It's not the money; it's the principle of the thing."

"Have you had any trouble with the police?" Julie asked.

"Nope, it's not illegal what I'm doing. This is America, land of the free
and home of the brave. I got the First Amendment on my side, even with
that socialist we got in the White House now. You can still speak your
piece, you know. And see, my sign says 'in my opinion.' That means the
dentist can't sue me for defamation. I'm not looking for aggro; I just want
what's mine. It's always the little people, the working people, that get
screwed in this country."

"Absolutely," agreed Julie. Then, remembering the "lawyerup" bill-
board she had seen, and the American propensity to sue, she asked, "Have
you thought of taking him to small claims court?"

"Nope, that wouldn't hurt him; he won't even show up in court. Standing here with my sign hurts him more. You see this place where he lives:
very exclusive, very upscale. These folks only drive a Mercedes or a Lexus;
they don't like their guests to have to pass me with my sign when they come
out for a day of golf. And next thing I'm going to do is track him down to
where he goes to church and take my signs over there."

Julie was impressed with the protestor's savvy tactics for resolving
his conflict. She thought about how differently people in other cultures

negotiated their disputes—through mediation and community participation, aiming for the reconciliation of all parties. Of course, that only
worked in face-to-face communities. In America's complex culture, this
guy might actually have the right idea. Ruining a dentist's reputation
with his social peers and potential patients might be the one thing that'd
get his attention.

  "Good luck," Julie wished him sincerely. "I hope you get your money
back." With a small wave she returned to the car, and she and Mike drove
off to the Wal-Mart, the next stop in her fieldwork.

Chapter Twenty-Four

"Oh, Mike, gorgeous day," Julie said as she flung open the terrace doors. "Perfect for the Everglades. Take a look at this map." Julie sat down and spread out her glossy map of South Florida on the large glass table. Mike leaned over her shoulder. "The Everglades are huge, Mike, and it's all different. Let's do Shark Valley today; that's only about twenty-five miles from here. We can rent bikes there; it's a fifteen-mile flat loop ride—lots of alligators who'll be looking for the sun after the cool weather. I'll make some sandwiches, and we'll just take some water. There's a local Miccosukee café on the canal where we can coffee up. You can drive there; it's a pretty straight shot on the Tamiami Trail"—she pointed her finger along the route—"which isn't too busy, and I'll drive back."

"Sounds good," Mike assented. After renting their bikes and completing the first six miles of the Shark Valley loop, they stopped by an alligator-filled pond near the park tower. Mike said to Julie with awe in his voice, "I've counted over fifty alligators already. They seem to be pretty social animals: look how they lay around with their faces flopped over their buddies' necks or their paws draped over the next guy's shoulders . . . would you call them 'shoulders' or what? This is a very moving experience, I kid you not."

Julie felt the same way. Even though she'd been here before camping with her parents, and had seen alligators in their several different habitats, she never failed to be amazed by them. *It's like being in one of those age-of-the-dinosaur films, but here the special effects aren't computer graphics; they're real.* Later, as they ate their lunch on a bench near the end of the bike loop, they were lucky enough to see a troop of black vultures stalking through the watery low grass, taking turns tearing up a fish, their rigid steps and black-masked faces giving them the serious look of medieval philosophers.

Outside the park boundaries, at Julie's directions, Mike pulled into the parking lot of the local Miccosukee diner whose neighbor was a general store advertising no-tax cigarettes. "I like to support Indian business," Julie turned to Mike, "but don't even think of buying Charlie a carton of cigarettes. I'll buy Kai some alligator souvenirs at one of their shops. Let's take a canal-side table at the café; maybe we'll see an Indian airboat ride pass by. We're best off with *iced* coffees; like everywhere else down here, their hot version is as tepid and weak as tea. I'll buy you a Sofkee; that's a warm, watery drink with the consistency of undercooked oatmeal and a fermented taste. You get your choice of rice or corn. You won't like it. But you only have to drink half of it. Eating strange food is an anthropological initiation into an indigenous culture. Get used to it."

The only other customer in the place was a lone Indian man, with a fiercely aquiline nose, deeply pitted skin, and very crooked teeth—*what there are of them*, both Julie and Mike noted, and under his soft, wide-brimmed black hat, he had a thick, black braid halfway down his back, tied with a ribbon. Julie and Mike walked their drinks to an outside table, enjoying the glorious breeze and wide sky now piling up a bit with clouds.

"I got some historical background on the Florida Indians off the time-share's computer," Julie said as she sipped her iced coffee. "The Miccosukees are the indigenous people around here. The Seminoles are farther north, more in central Florida—they're different tribes, but their problems are pretty similar. First, it's their dying environment, a case of 'water, water everywhere but not a drop to drink.' Housing construction, commercial development, agribusiness—that's mostly big sugar protectionism down here—tariffs on cheaper foreign sugar, and subsidies to our own industry have killed off millions of acres of wetlands throughout Florida since the early 1900s. That guy Flagler has a lot to answer for to the Indians . . . Florida is literally dying from the *scale* of its development. And even though it provides some jobs, a lot of the local people don't really benefit.

"Like in the sugar industry, up around Belle Glade—they don't pay a living wage, so they can't get locals to do the backbreaking work, even though the black male unemployment rate down here is through the roof. That gives the companies the excuse they need to hire immigrant labor through the H2-A visa program. If those folks even think about fighting back, the corporations just deport them. They even had a slavery case against them; that was back around World War II. Things have improved a little. A Palm Beach judge just ruled that the Florida sugar cane companies owe thousands of workers over $50 million for having cheated them out of their wages over the last five years. But that's peanuts to them compared to the companies' subsidized profits. I tell you, if Americans knew where their sugar really comes from and its cost in human misery, maybe it would cut down the national obesity problem. But it's a well-kept secret. You think any tourists, or even local Floridians, ever go to Belle Glade?"

"I can see the problem, Julie, just from where I'm sitting: that Indian guy out there, and he's not so old either, with practically no teeth; and overweight waitresses with bad skin and unhealthy diets, making peanuts I'm sure. Even if they have a souvenir shop, let's face it: their old way of life is dead, and they haven't worked up to their place in a modern economy. I've read enough about the Indian reservations out West to know what the employment market is for those guys. Why would it be any different down here?"

"Exactly the problem, Mike. Their way of life demanded land and fresh water, and the vegetation and animals it supported, but just like out West, they couldn't sustain it once the settlers moved in. Then the corporations got into the saddle. The housing for working people eats up a lot of the land, but what really hurts is the spread of the more affluent developments, like the gated communities: everybody wanting a water view and digging canals—now they're full of alligators people bought for pets and threw away after they blew out the birthday candles. And the fish are full of mercury. But you still get some Indians and other folks fishing them for food, not fun. Then the state 'improved'"—Julie made air quotes here—"the inland waterway for boat owners, so now there are more manatee deaths than ever despite speed rules. Can you believe it, Mike? There are people who deliberately harass and kill these most inoffensive of animals— they're sea cows, for goodness sake; they munch out the vegetation in the waterways. Well, they're practically extinct, even though there's a Save the Manatee Club that lobbies for protected status and other laws that will keep them from totally disappearing.

"Unlike the Indians, most of the immigrants in Florida are relatively urbanized," Julie explained, "so they can carve out communities from aging and decaying housing clusters that earlier residents have abandoned. Eventually, some of them prosper and move; others stay and improve their communities, but a lot of them have their communities improved or gentrified out from under them. Meanwhile, high-rises or gated communities are newly built farther and farther up the coast. It takes a ton of fresh water to keep this bubble from bursting, but it's too late for the Indians.

"Even this natural wonderland of the Everglades helped do in the Indians." Julie's expression conveyed sadness at the thought. "Let's face it, even you and I are part of the problem. Who do you think lost their land to protect this unique environment? Great for us: hiking, biking, canoeing—wait'll you see Bear Creek; you'll think you died and went to heaven—spoonbills, huge, prehistoric-looking wood ibises, just fabulous. But this was land essential to the Indian way of life. Don't get me wrong, better it should be a protected national park than sucked up into private development. All these Florida officials courting the corporations, oil drilling, agribusiness, playing political footsie. They're even starting to privatize some of the Florida beaches. That used to be totally off limits; beaches were open to everyone, but under the hat even that's changing. Sure the feds are finally chipping in with some relatively big bucks to save what's left. An Everglades Restoration Act passed more than a decade ago, but the political-industrial muscle made sure it would be 'studied' to death. And if you think 'restored' means back to its original condition, *forget about it.* Big sugar won't give up its land. Pratt and Whitney are being sued for contaminating the water in West Palm Beach—they call it a 'cancer cluster' now—but they'll settle out of court eventually, and meanwhile your loved one is dead or dying from cancer."

"Haven't they heard about the greening of America?" Mike asked. "There must be people in Florida sensitive to that issue. It would be in their own best interest, wouldn't it?"

"I don't want to sound cynical, Mike," Julie scoffed, "but if you read the ads in those glossy magazines at the time-share, you'll see what 'green' means down here. '*Pistachio-green home appointments*'—that's a quote: plumbing fixtures with hand-painted *green* butterflies, a $7,700 credenza painted *avocado green.* This stuff's aimed at the same folks who still buy gas guzzlers and take out lifetime memberships for golf courses that consume more water than the Indians ever drank up in four centuries. Well, don't get me started."

"You mean this was all a preamble? You haven't gotten started yet, Julie?" Mike laughed good-naturedly. "Come on; let's get some of those alligator souvenirs."

When their shopping was done, Julie popped into the driver's seat and told Mike that they were going to pass by "a current solution to Indian poverty. I want to get your take on it. Remember I told you there were two separate Indian nations, the Seminoles and the Miccosukee, that were really done in by Florida land reclamation and diversion of water for development uses and so on? Well, an anthropologist from UCLA just wrote a book on the Seminoles where she examines the cultural, economic, and political aspects of casino gambling—oh, 'scuse me," Julie minced her tone sarcastically, "it's not *gambling*; that smacks of the bad old days of mob control, exploiting people's addiction, whatever. The current term is 'gaming.' So the Seminoles's $25 million *gaming* revenues bought them input into the Everglades restoration project I mentioned before. They believe—I'm paraphrasing here—'If our land dies, our tribe will die too.' So hopefully, they'll put pressure on to max the restoration.

"Now the Miccosukee are also using legal gambling to further their tribal interests. They became an officially recognized tribe in the sixties, when there was a lot of support for ethnic pride. The recognition gave them more control over their future because they could administer their own tribal affairs instead of going through the Indian Bureau. They set up their own departments of education, public safety, and health and were given help in creating tribal businesses like we saw today: shops, tourist attractions outside the park, an Indian village re-creation. They've also managed to hold on to their language to some degree and retain their clan structure, and they still celebrate a traditional spring corn festival. A Miccosukee Indian, name of Buffalo Tiger, an old guy who learned English, represented the tribe in a lot of its dealings with the government. He pioneered Indian-style cultural activities to attract the tourists and became the go-to man at the center of the Miccosukee gaming industry. Apparently, some Indians are against him for modernizing too fast. They feel that if the Indians would keep the old ways more strictly, the young kids wouldn't be falling into the drug and alcohol problems they have now. But Buffalo Tiger argues that at least he's kept some aspects of the Miccosukee culture alive. And with the huge revenues from legal gambling, they'll have the money to fight the social ills. So let's take a look," Julie concluded as she pulled into the huge parking lot of the Krome Avenue gambling palace.

"Not too busy yet," Mike observed, as he looked across the almost empty lot to the Disneyland-style high-rise casino hotel painted white, turquoise, and pink. "Probably too early. Mostly retired folks at this time of day, I'd guess." He scanned the glossy brochure Julie had passed to him. "But they call it a resort, so it must get a family crowd. Introduce the kiddies to 'gaming' as soon as they're tall enough to pull a lever," he added. "I don't know, Julie; maybe this is one of those 'victimless crimes' I still haven't made up my mind about."

"Me neither, Mike. I never gamble; it's not a morality thing with me, but the few times I tried, I never won. Oh, yeah, once I won a frying pan at a bingo game on those special Florida trains my mom and I used to take when we visited Aunt Lottie without Dad. The Gold Coast's changed a lot since then, and these Indian gambling casinos are a big part of it."

As Julie got out of the car, she directed Mike's attention to a bright red Mercedes hardtop convertible nearby with the plate LUCKYLOU. "Hey, you're right about the retirees here. See, that's Lou's car. I told you I noticed it on the way to Gert's office, and she said it was his. You remember Lou?"

"The saint?" Mike finished for her. "Yeah. Unless senility is catching, I remember everything you say. Do you want to say hello or what?"

"I do Mike, just for a minute. That guy he's with is dragging his leg; he must be Lou's new gambling crony. Gert told me they're off to the races, Jai Lai, or the casinos a lot. Lou, Lou," Julie yelled out and waved her hand. Lou came over as soon as he recognized her and embraced her. "Julie, Julie, I'm glad I can give you my condolences in person. I know you were over your aunt's place. Gert told me you came by. You know me and Sol; we were best buddies, and your aunt, too. She could be pretty prickly some-times, but hey, life dealt her a few blows."

"You were a good friend, Lou, and Mom and I never forget it. Here's a friend of mine, Mike Cardella. Mike, Lou Freedman. I've told you about him." The men shook hands as Lou's friend limped over. He ignored Julie and Mike but tapped Lou on the shoulder in a way that suggested he didn't want to enter the conversation. "I wanna try that high-stakes bingo; you can find me there." Lou took hold of his arm before he could limp away. "Hey, Kenny, just a minute. This is my old friend Julie; she's an anthropol-ogist from New York, and this is her friend Mike." Kenny squinted at Julie for a few seconds, and then quickly muttered, "Yeah, well, have a nice visit. I'll see ya upstairs, Lou." As he limped away, Lou said, "Okay, Julie, so he's not your Uncle Sol. I loved that guy. He wouldn't gamble high stakes like Kenny, but he always brought me luck. Kenny's not a bad fella, has some kind of job at North Miami Gen, where you visited Aunt Lottie so many times, may she rest in peace. He's like a counselor for people who want to donate their organs or something like that. You wouldn't think it to look at him, but he's good company, always ready for an adventure. Not one single guy is alive and kicking from the old building, can you believe it?"

"I can, Lou. But it's great to see you in good health and high spirits. Get out there and win!" Julie hugged him goodbye. She turned back to the car and fished out another resort brochure from the front seat. "I want to make sure we cover all the 'attractions,' Mike; that's how they advertise them. The sports bar means big-screen boxing matches; first-rate musical entertainment means Las Vegas showgirls, but it's all low cost since those are just the enticements to gamble. Can you imagine? That bingo game Kenny was running off to goes on all night long: 'Early Bird to Insomnia,'" she read aloud. As they passed a larger-than-life bronze statue of a Miccosukee woman in traditional tribal appliqué clothing, Julie recalled to Mike the handmade Indian patchwork hat and jacket her parents had bought her here when she was a little girl, and which she had saved to this day. As they passed the Indian shop's window in the ornate casino lobby, Julie noted the high-quality craftwork displayed and the equally high prices on the tags. "I hope the winners shop till they drop here," she said to Mike. "Maybe it won't save the part of Miccosukee culture that's passed away, but at least it might help keep alive a remnant for the grandchildren."

☘ Chapter Twenty-Five

"Big day, today, Mike. Zumba class is at ten, and don't pull that long face. We'll work up our appetite for a delicious lunch downtown, and then we're going to Overton in the afternoon."

The time-share van took them over to a local hall where the Zumba class was being held. Even though they were a little early, the place was packed when they arrived. "Not your usual golf crowd," Mike observed agreeably as he looked over the diverse mob. They were mostly in their twenties and thirties but with a sprinkling of "really old folks," too, Julie pointed out. The participants were dressed in every kind of outfit imaginable. "Street cool," Mike noted, as he surveyed the many young men wearing fedoras or bandanas, and tank tops; a lot of them with full arm and calf tattoos; and the girls wearing tummy-baring Lycra tops, form-fitting leggings, and high-topped sneakers. They were all staking out their spots as the instructor, a young woman in a black jumpsuit that looked painted on her muscular body, greeted everyone with a broad smile. As she was putting on the music—a fast afro-salsa beat to get the crowd warmed up—Julie whispered a little instruction to Mike, warning him that once the music started the beat would become so fast they wouldn't be able to speak until it was over. Following the leader's moves, shaking every part of his body without poking his extended arms into his neighbor's eye, and wiping the sweat out of his eyes halfway through, Mike admitted afterward it'd been great fun and terrific exercise.

"All started by an overweight UPS truck driver in Ohio with a yen for music who decided to skip his fattening fast food lunches and spend the hour dancing in his truck in a supermarket parking lot instead," Julie filled Mike in. "His overweight wife joined him and easily recruited a group of friends to their basement den a couple of nights a week. The next thing was to rent a hall, and then go high tech with a professional DVD. It made millions! I do love to see the American entrepreneurial system at work."

"Yeah, me, too," Mike agreed, and then with a pleading look asked Julie, "Now can I sit in the hot tub back at the ranch?"

"Yeah, we have some time," Julie okayed. "Go soak. We're meeting Eric for lunch in that new restaurant in the Design District, and then he's going to take us for a tour of Overton. The restaurant's a little pricey, but we don't qualify for the senior citizen early bird discount."

"Hey, we *would* qualify for that now, Julie. I wasn't a senior citizen when I came down here, but with all our investigations, time-share activities, the Everglades, your fieldwork, and now Zumba, I'm beginning to feel like one. Think we'll have any time to relax after tonight?"

"Time to relax is in the casket, Mike. Let's enjoy ourselves. Carpe diem."

Julie followed the MapQuest directions to the Design District and located the restaurant without any problem. Eric was waiting inside, at a canal-side table; although they had only spoken with Eric on the phone, they had no trouble recognizing him from Barry and Dom's description. After they all shook hands, and sat down to enjoy the view of the wading birds and the alligators, Mike growled, "If the food's as good as the view, I'll have no complaint." After they ordered, Julie turned to Eric and thanked him for all the information he had given them in their phone conversation.

Mike added his thanks and then said enthusiastically, "Now, I want to hear all about Overton. Julie said you grew up there, and it's a very special place. I'd never heard of it."

"Very few white people heard of Overton," Eric said. "And it is a special place but not the kind of special place most tourists visit, or at least white tourists. Or it didn't used to be.

"It has an interesting history, though. It's one of the oldest neighborhoods in Miami. In the late 1890s, when Flagler built his railroad here, he needed a place for his workers to live. Jim Crow kept the blacks from most established neighborhoods in South Florida, so Miami west of Flagler's railroad tracks became 'Colored Town.' Like a lot of other black communities across the States, it was a really dynamic place, even if it was poor. They had schools, churches, and a lot of black businesses, everything from barbershops to grocery and furniture stores. A hot music scene, too, and theaters and nightclubs—not exactly the Harlem Renaissance but an exciting place in many ways. Black celebrities came here: Count Basie, Cab Calloway, and Nat King Cole, and black scholars, too, like Zora Neale Hurston and W. E. B. DuBois. Those days, it didn't matter how high you rose professionally; it was 'if you're black, stay back'—all over the country, not just in Florida. So a lot of the black elite from all over shook the cold by taking their vacations in Overton. Eventually, a lot of the middle-class blacks moved out, but there's still a real community feel to the place.

"In the 1980s, there were race riots here. An all-white jury had acquitted some white police officers who beat a black insurance salesman to death. Some of the local residents took revenge by dragging several whites from their cars and beating or burning *them* to death. Not a good time."

"I heard things are getting a little better now," Julie offered. "Is that true, Eric?"

"Well, it's still poor, and white American tourists still stay away. And it still has a reputation for being dangerous. There's been a movement on for development, but so far it's mostly fits and starts, demolishing housing and displacing residents without getting much rebuilt. Lately, though, a real renaissance seems to be starting; let's see where it goes. They're landmarking lots of the historic churches and other old buildings, like the Black Police Precinct. That might interest you, Mike; it's an architectural beauty. The legendary Lyric Theatre was closed down for a while, but that's reopening too."

"I read about the Art Basel festival, Eric," Julie added. "It seems to be bringing Overton back to life. The *Times* had a big spread on the murals of an Overton artist, a real street person named Purvis Young. They call him an outsider artist; he made a big splash in Miami where his work is becoming a big tourist attraction."

"There's also lots of boring middle-class, suburban-type houses with swimming pools, but it's no Coral Gables yet. The problem is the homeless living in cardboard huts under the highway ramps are still there, too. Blame I-95 again, white Florida's expressways breaking up solid black city centers."

"Florida's a funny place," Julie reflected aloud. "There *is* a lot of cultural diversity on the Gold Coast, lots of different ethnic enclaves, and even among the ethnic groups, there are distinct communities. The blacks have Overton and Liberty City, but there is also the Haitian area, like the one near my aunt's ALF. Same with the different Spanish-speaking groups: Cubans, of course, in Little Havana, but Colombians elsewhere and migrant Mexicans up around Pompano. The Cubans run politics, but things are changing there, too. About fifteen years ago when the Cuban dance band Los Van Van performed in Miami, thousands of rock- and bottle-throwing Cuban demonstrators outnumbered the concertgoers. But last year, the group performed without any problems. All the mayor was concerned about was to keep the traffic moving. A few exile groups still protested, but the Cubans have become a little more politically moderate now. The tourist industry, along with the medical industry, is *b-i-i-i-g* down here: music, sports, cultural diversity, whatever it takes—when money talks, politics walks!"

Here Mike broke in, "But you don't see it in the street life, like in New York. Maybe that's because there's so little street life here. Nobody walks; everybody drives."

"And speaking of driving," Julie said with a smile, "as soon as Mike pays the check, we're going to get in our car, drive to Overton, and walk our feet off so everyone will know we're from New York!"

Chapter Twenty-Six

Miami, January 11, 2010

When Julie's cell phone chirped, she motioned Mike to pause the *CSI: Miami* DVD they were watching. "Hey, Ernesto, *que tal*? Yeah, Mike's sitting right here. I'll put him on."

"Hey, *amigo*," Ernesto's deep, rich voice chuckled. "We serve and protect by keeping our cells on 24-7. I only called Julie 'cause I couldn't raise you." Mike grinned and listened for a moment, and then turned to Julie. "Tomorrow lunch at the Versailles at two, okay? Ernesto says, 'Bring a fork, this turkey's done.'"

"I'm gonna recap everything from when you were down here last year," Ernesto began soberly once they'd given their orders. "I haven't kept you up to date for a while because the investigation wasn't going in a straight line. Remember last June, at lunch, I told you about Linda's mom's death going along one track: elderly women with similar profiles; it had to be some medical guy, maybe this Dr. Galbinki she suspected, who'd attended all of them. But we had no concrete evidence, *nada*. And there was an overlap with other suspicious hospital deaths where the victim profiles were off: men—young, middle aged, brain dead, or on life support—and unexpected or unexplained deaths that had come into Miami Homicide via family complaints. Several of them referred to some guy from an organ donation firm who acted pretty pushy; plus most of these bodies were sent off to the same funeral home, Comfort Providers. It was looking maybe like two different perps at work. One is ours; the other seems like what the mystery books call a red herring.

"So first we separated the elderly women like Linda's mom and Julie's aunt from Homicide's list. They kept us in the loop on their investigation. They had the manpower to interview all the hospital personnel at North Miami General: doctors, nurses, orderlies, caregivers, and administrators—the only ones they left out were the priests and the rabbis—anyone who worked where most of their suspected victims had died. A thankless job, catching hundreds of medical workers on their different shifts; we were glad that was their patch.

"Homicide fingered a few possible perps. One of them—some dude named Eric—they found had been left money by a lot of the folks he worked for."

"Yeah, we met the guy," Mike and Julie interrupted simultaneously. "He took us around Overton—definitely one of the good guys."

"Right, he was a nonstarter. Then Homicide tapped another guy for us, a Kenny Conners; he's an organ donor counselor—did you ever hear of such a job? North Miami Gen is in his territory, and he's weird. First, Homicide tells us, he's cooperative. Then they get under his skin, and he's defensive. 'I just do my job; anybody says something else, they're lying.' Then he shuts up. The Homicide guys run down our list of death dates— Linda's mom, Julie's aunt, and some other elderly women we've had reports on—and stick it under his nose. They quiz him on his whereabouts for those days. Bang! He explodes. The mutt pulls out a fistful of gambling tickets from a manila envelope he's carrying—Jai Alai, dog track, Indian casinos—and slaps them on the table. 'I got tickets, all date stamped,' he yells. 'I got alibis: my friend Lucky Lou; we stick together. I never play without him. Check it out.' Okay," Ernesto continued, "so the Homicide guys do check 'em out, running down every date; they call this Lucky Lou—a righteous guy it turns out, respectable pharmacist."

"Ernesto!" Julie again burst into his narrative. "This is so strange. That's my Aunt Lottie's and Uncle Sol's best friend since they moved down here. He defines righteous—never bets more than he can afford to lose and helps the old ladies do their grocery shopping—a saint. I introduced him to Mike last year at the Miccosukee casino resort; he was with this same weird guy, this Kenny. You remember, Mike?"

Mike smiled good-naturedly. "I keep telling you, Julie. Alzheimer's isn't contagious. Of course I remember."

"What a coincidence," Ernesto shook his head disbelievingly. "Anyway, put aside this Kenny's bizarre stunt waving around his gambling stubs. He's got solid alibis for all of our elderly women's deaths—end of that story, too bad on us. But I'm gonna take a minute to wrap up Homicide's case for you before I move on to ours because I think you'll find it interesting. See, the murder boys aren't ready to toss this guy Kenny just yet. They wanna see now if he connects to *their* file of complaints made to Gold Coast hospitals about suspicious or unexpected deaths. They start back a year, January 1, 2009. *Bingo*, there's a suspicious death complaint against North Miami Gen for just that date. What a way to celebrate the New Year, huh? The complaint was made by the cousin of a guy who was in his midfifties, in a coma, but with a good prognosis, who had unexpectedly died of 'natural causes.' The guy's cousin flies down to Miami and goes right to North Miami Gen to wring specific cause of death info out of the attending doctor. He doesn't buy the vague explanation that his cousin's 'system just collapsed.' His official complaint also included some hell-raising about the Comfort Providers Funeral Home, where the hospital had sent the deceased. It seems its director had called this cousin to suggest immediate cremation, which the family refused to even consider. But when the cousin was told he couldn't prosecute for wrongful death in Florida unless he exhumed the body and authorized a full autopsy with drug screen, it was too much for him. So the complaint petered out, end of that story.

"Meanwhile, standard procedure, Homicide subpoenas Kenny's cell records, just to see what floats to the top, and again, New Year's Eve night, like 4:00 a.m., they find two calls, each under a minute, to Comfort Providers Funeral Home." Ernie raised his eyebrows. "What, Kenny's discussing his golf scores in the wee hours of party night? Not likely. But the mutt yaks his way through some wrong number BS, and without any probable cause Homicide can't hold him.

"But then the murder guys grab the brass ring. They're reinterviewing some Haitian college kid. He's a part-time newbie orderly working nights at the hospital to keep afloat; he was on duty New Year's Eve. Now the kid admits he saw something. He didn't say anything the first time 'cause it was a guy in a white coat—looked like a doctor—maybe doing some special treatment or whatever with a patient, and who was he to interfere; he didn't want to jeopardize his job by whistle-blowing—weak excuse maybe but understandable. He tells Homicide he got a clear view of a guy, limping slow, dragging his leg, and stopping to check the doorplates of each room by the overhead corridor lights. Homicide shows him a photo array, and with no hesitation, he fingers their mutt, Kenny. They hold a lineup, no problem for the kid. 'That leg, I couldn't mistake him.' The interview and lineup are gold, videotaped; now Homicide's got more than probable cause, yadda, yadda, yadda. Their investigation really hots up.

"Then sometime in April, the murder squad gets a tip: guy with a Spanish accent at a pay phone. They couldn't get there in time, but he's telling them that he was just paid to pick up a sealed cooler in the middle of the night at the Comfort Providers Funeral Home and drive it to the airport. He describes the guy who paid him and spouts the car make, model, and license number. Homicide goes right to Kenny's cell phone records again—they have the date, so they don't have to go blind on the lists this time. Clear as day, two under-a-minute calls to Comfort Providers, right to the funeral director's line itself. Now they're in business. They've got the muscle to bring the FBI, the IRS, whatever they need. They tear the place apart—people are lucky their loved ones weren't carted away with the cartons of files. Down in the sub-basement there's a room full of slabs and the equipment for tissue removal and you don't wanna know what else. Case closed: just a couple of greedy bastards, gambling debts, living large, whatever—a gorier scam than most down here, but you've read Roubicek's book. For some folks, it's money counts, forget anything else. Organ and tissue sales; it's great ink these days: the good guys win this round in court and in the press. Unfortunately, it doesn't add anything to our investigation. But it gets the red herring out of the way and lets us focus."

Ernesto checked his watch. "Julie, you got time for a coco flan, right?" Julie nodded firmly. "And I'll have my *own* New York cheesecake flan," Mike mock whined. "Last time, Julie didn't really share."

After Ernesto gave their orders, including a flan of his own, he continued his story. "So now we're really into our solo investigation, but I just want to make one point first. Mike, remember when you first came down, on that Santeria nutcase murder? I told you about how Miami-Dade policing really reaches out into the communities, Haitians, Mexicans, Guatemalans, Cubans, of course, some Colombians—mostly drugs but you never know— even some scattered Peruvians, whatever, and the different ethnic groups within each nationality, different religious affiliations, you name it. We're out there. Got our CIs, our elder abuse squad, a bunch of task force leaders, teenage programs, and language facilities; we hold community-police meetings, and we build trust any way we can. You're gonna see; it paid off.

"Okay, so, Linda's mom: that's our strongest case. It couldn't have been Galbinki's first; it was too organized for that. We trawl our earlier reports of suspicious deaths of elderly women, like that Sylvia Stein story Charlotte told you last year, where the granddaughter suspected Galbinki of stealing from her grandmother's jewelry pouches. Another case involving Galbinki came from a little farther up the Gold Coast, some feisty old New Yorker, wouldn't you know, who was the contact person for an elderly lady friend with no close relatives. He'd registered a complaint with the hospital about the unexpected and suspicious death of this woman whose illness hadn't seemed so serious, but without official standing, he couldn't get anywhere. You see, down here, with the over eighties and an attending doctor certifying death from 'natural causes,' nothing's gonna happen unless family or the physician himself pushes for a full, drug screen autopsy. Obviously, Galbinki being this lady's doctor, and possibly her killer—he won't ask for it. So the medical examiner can't do it on the taxpayers' dime, and the deceased lady has no money, so it slides. And we're still left with Linda's mom as our best hope to keep the good doctor from getting away with murder.

"But what's his motive for her murder, a breakfront full of Barbie dolls and crap like that? Money, juries understand. But Galbinki doesn't kill for money. So why does he put himself in a trickbag by *forging* Lillian's will? That's what did him in. He had to know our handwriting experts could prove the signature's a fake. He left two dicey witnesses to the will; he had to realize we'd trace them eventually, which we did. They both nailed him in a photo array and admitted he'd given them twenty bucks for their signatures— 'nothing that would get them in trouble,' he'd assured them. Why would he bother?" Ernesto frowned. "Most people don't know this, but legally, motive isn't necessary to make a case. But without it, a lot of prosecutors are afraid of losing. Motive helps jurors feel more comfortable about convicting. So we keep working on that. We think, if we can get to a motive for Lillian's death, it'll indicate motive for all the rest if we ever charge on them.

"Anyway, we want Lillian's case as airtight as possible. We start the uniforms on a door-to-door in her building; that's where our community-policing outreach really worked its mojo. They turn up a family: man's a decent working stiff, legal; his wife, too; and a teenage daughter, Angela, born here, smart kid. She walked Lillian's dogs and really liked her. Good people, going after the American dream the right way. But the guy's got his young sister and her baby living with them, undocumented, very little English. Angela tells the uniforms that she wants a detective who speaks Spanish, one of the special *policia* Lillian told her about that takes care of the old people, calls them up every morning to see they're still alive. That's actually not us . . ." Ernesto began to explain, but Julie cut him off. "Not necessary, Ernesto, I know about these Senior Watch calls; they were a highlight of Aunt Lottie's mornings."

"Okay, good," Ernesto continued. "So, Angela gets to me eventually, says her young aunt may have some information, but she's nervous about the cops; they'll send her back to Mexico. I assure her that won't happen. Her aunt's a valuable witness in a serial homicide case; let's hear what she has to say. She tells a straightforward, credible story. The night Lillian was killed, she's coming into the building about 9:30 with her crying baby at the same time as a tall, well-dressed man, *Americano*, she's sure; she got a close look at him. She's afraid he's visiting some grumpy, old relative who'll come out in the hallway to complain about the baby's crying. *Buena suerte*, nobody opens their door, and she hurries to her brother's apartment down the hallway. To put her key in the lock, she has to turn the baby around, and she gets another real good look at this guy entering 'the third apartment,' as she tells Angela, who knows that's Lillian's apartment. The brother says, 'forget it, we play dumb and go about our business.' Angela confirms there was no complaint about the noise that night because Gert, the landlady, would have passed it on.

"So," Ernesto paused to dig into his flan, "we return with a photo array, all by the book; the sister picks Galbinki out right away. Along with the forged will, the DA's willing to charge Galbinki with Lillian's murder. Linda arranges for the exhumation of her mom's body; that takes a little time. No cemetery, especially Arlington, full of patriots and tourists who come to honor them, is happy about digging up graves. And it's very expensive. But the DA gets funds for a nighttime exhumation, and Linda pays for a separate autopsy in addition to one by our medical examiner, who's aces, just to make doubly sure of any results. Both autopsies find traces of succinylcholine sufficient to kill; it's a chemical with no reason at all for being in Lillian's body. There's our case. The sister with the baby, speaking through an expert translator, is strong support. Unfortunately, with all this CSI forensics stuff on TV, the human element, like eyewitness testimony, has been put in the shade, but it's still important for us.

"And by now," Ernesto pursed his lips reflectively, "with our own interrogations, collaboration with FBI profilers, and lots of different law enforcement specialists, we've figured out motive. Galbinki is your garden-variety sociopath, a serial killer whose motive is inside his head. There's where we have to look."

"A serial killer—it sounds so far-fetched," Julie interrupted Ernesto.

"Shouldn't," he replied abruptly. "Statistically, and in terms of personality profiles, serial killing is as American as apple pie. Rich ones like Galbinki sometimes skate because they can afford the biggest lawyers. But sometimes even the best lawyers can't zip a client's lips. Sociopaths aren't just predators. Many need to get their superiority in your face; they just can't help showing their contempt, for their victims, for the cops, for the whole judicial system. That's what motivates them. Galbinki's like that; you'll see. Maybe he'll overplay his hand if we can get him on the stand. See, in our first interview, he smirks at me, 'Detective, have you ever read Nietzsche?'"

"The superior man to whom society's rules don't apply," Mike responded, knowing where Ernesto was going with this.

"Right," Ernesto agreed, "but I didn't know it then. Some Nazi philosopher, I found out later. The doc lectures me a little: how some men are above the masses, and physicians especially hold the keys to life and death in their hands—superior intelligence, yadda, yadda, yadda. I let him talk.

"Then he starts in about 'these Florida widows.' Why are we making such a fuss about them, low, vulgar women who've had more than their share, nagging and spending their weak-willed husbands into their graves. 'Do you know about Jung's theory of archetypes?' he asks my partner Luis. See, I'm invisible already, the *idiota* who can't talk philosophy with him. But Luis knows Jung; he's a college man like Mike here. He and Galbinki have a pleasant, high-toned conversation. It appears that Galbinki's mother is the archetype he despises, a woman who beat his father down with her constant demands. Galbinki's enjoying this now, bonding with Luis; we play it for all it's worth—and get an earful. How his mother killed his father's spirit by ridiculing his high moral standards, his boasts that he never cheated a customer. How she buried him in their hideous sweatshop, forcing him to squeeze every penny out of their workers and cook the books for the IRS. Even in public she cursed him as a fool. 'I had to agree with her there,' Galbinki confides to Luis, who seconds the motion that only fools operate ethically in our corrupt society. Galbinki blames his father that he never protested, just sucked up everything his mother dished out. When the old man finally, *actually* died, he and 'Mother' moved out of their jerkwater town to the Gold Coast, where Galbinki started his lucrative medical career. 'And what did I find here but carbon copies of Mother,' he complained to Luis, who nodded sympathetically. When our squad reviewed the tape, it gave us a handle on the pattern of his victims and how specific events in his own life might have acted as traumatic triggers. The picture became even clearer when we got up to Singer Island to visit *mamacita*. Galbinki knew his onions about rich Florida widows; I'll give him that. A mansion with three glitzy vehicles in the drive, and she was haughty as hell—tried to leave us on the doorstep like something she brought in on the bottom of her shoe. Our bird didn't fall far from that nest.

"So now we think we do have motive if we can shoehorn it in. It was never the money. The doc owns a huge plantation house on the intercoastal waterway, has his own pier and boat. Lillian's collectibles and the jewelry he snitched didn't mean squat to him; they were just trophies of his ability to manipulate and kill as he pleased. Blondie, his current receptionist girlfriend, told us he'd occasionally given her some impressive piece of jewelry whose inscription to another woman made her wonder. But he always explained it away by saying a beloved great aunt or whoever had told him to bestow it on a special lady in his life. Blondie confessed that after the first couple of presents she didn't really believe this, but who was she to look her gift horse in the mouth. No standing by her man for that broad."

"So, Ernesto, do *you* think Aunt Lottie was another of Galbinki's victims?" Julie asked tentatively. "Nurse Mendelsohn's account of my aunt's last night alive seemed to implicate him, but Mike thought it might not stand up as proof."

"That's about right," Ernie conceded sadly. "It would be a hard charge to prove unless you'd have her body exhumed and autopsied for traces of a lethal substance. Would you do that?"

Julie hesitated. "No, I don't think so, and I know one close relative who would be absolutely against it. When Galbinki is convicted on Lillian's death, he can only serve one life sentence anyway. Convicting him twice won't bring Aunt Lottie back." Julie paused. "Just one more thing, though, Ernesto . . . my aunt's diamond heart . . . is there a chance . . . ?"

"In your hands as we speak, Julie." Ernesto slipped a small black velvet box across the table. "This is no longer in our chain of evidence against Galbinki. Our mass murdering doctor *will* get life without parole on Lillian's death, and in Florida that means just what it says—plus four years for forging the will. That's a laugh, isn't it?" Ernesto didn't laugh.

Epilogue

January 13, 2010

"Many Feared Dead as Huge Earthquake Strikes Haiti: Rescue Operation Under Way for Victims in Rubble."

"Fierce Quake Devastates Haiti. Fears of Huge Death Toll."

"Ferocious Earthquake Rocks Haiti. People Are Out in the Streets, Crying, Screaming, Shouting."

"Donations Pour in for Victims of Haitian Earthquake."

Georgie heard the news and saw the headlines. *I gotta go*, he thought. *There must be something I can do.*

🌴 Acknowledgments

Our deepest appreciation goes to the many people who assisted us in our research and offered their support in the writing of this book: Susie Avnet and Ronald Gill; Judith Barbanel; Ric Broberg and the Boca Raton PAL; Douglas Feldman; Robert Fox; Juan Gallardo; Steve Geffrard; Ora and Myron Gelberg; Ken and Karen Glotzer; Alan Huffman; Barry and Janet Kass; Ira Kluger; Lillian Kristal; Jack Meinhardt; Jill Norgren; Beth Pacheco; Marissa Parks; Detective Joe Roubicek; David Schreier; Philippa Strum; Mary Winslow; Gwen Thomson and the Department of Anthropology, the John Jay College of Criminal Justice; and the Faculty Resource Center staff at New York City Technical College, City University of New York. Very special thanks to Floyd and Beth Miller, Toby and Senator Tom Dowd, and Jay and Eva Sexter. We would also like to acknowledge the assistance of our editors at AltaMira Press—Wendi Schnaufer, Marissa Parks, and Patricia Stevenson—in seeing this book through to completion.

🌴 Discussion Questions

1. The American Dream, a core theme of American culture, is presented through the life stories of different characters, such as Georgie (chapter 1); Aunt Lottie (chapter 2); Frankie and Arlene (chapter 5); Howie (chapter 9); Lillian (chapter 11); Rhoda and her dad, Dom (chapters 21 and 22); Dr. Galbinki (chapter 11); and Manuel (chapter 13). What is the American Dream? What are some of the similarities and differences among these characters and how they achieved their American Dream? In what ways has the American Dream been part of your life?

2. Culture is a central concept in our story. How would you describe the core American cultural values and norms? Using evidence from various chapters, discuss how these values and norms (for example, individualism, pragmatism, volunteerism, social mobility, the pursuit of personal happiness, and others) are overtly and implicitly illustrated through the attitudes, dialogue, and behavior of the characters in our story. In your opinion, is there an American culture? A Florida culture? A "car culture" (chapter 10)? Does the region you live in have a "culture"? What features does it share with the larger culture, and what are some important differences?

3. As an anthropologist, Julie uses ethnography to gain insights into American and South Floridian culture. She conducts fieldwork, for example, through close observation of sites of American/Floridian

culture (e.g., chapters 4 and 9); participation in social networks and activities (chapter 24); reflections on and analyses of ordinary behavior and popular media such as television (chapter 5); focused conversations with selected informants (chapters 22 and 23); and comparisons of American/Floridian culture and that of other societies (chapters 3, 12, and 15). In your view, how does ethnography offer a useful method of revealing American culture? What are some special difficulties in doing ethnography in one's own culture?

4. The idea of the "man in the white coat" (chapters 1 and 13) questions the right of anthropologists to "meddle" in the donation and trade of human organs and tissues. Today, an activist approach to applying social scientific knowledge to contemporary problems is a major direction of anthropology and other social sciences (e.g., chapters 10 and 24). How, if at all, do you think social scientists should become actively involved in addressing social problems, such as the relation of global poverty to illness and disease; the legal or illegal trade in human organs and tissues; the exploitation of the elderly; federal or local government policies on immigration; environmental destruction; or issues involving diverse ethnic communities, such as Native American casino gambling?

5. Both mainstream American and subcultural attitudes toward aging and eldercare (e.g., chapters 3, 7, and 16) are central to our story. Using examples in the text, describe these aspects of American culture and society that have important impacts on aging and eldercare, such as gender roles, retirement options, medical culture, and economics. How do these compare with other cultures?

6. Eldercare in the United States is gendered, and largely privatized, outsourced, and globalized: in addition to care by families, it increasingly includes part- or full-time caregivers in the home, most of whom are women, and immigrant workers, both documented and undocumented, as well as different types of for-profit and publicly supported residential institutions (e.g., chapters 6, 7, 16, and 17). From your knowledge or experience with any of these alternatives, what are their pros and cons? How has globalization impacted American eldercare?

7. Discuss the "medical culture" in the United States—that is, the values and norms specific to the health professions (e.g., chapters 4, 14, 17, and 19). How does the American medical culture relate to eldercare? What are some of the different views about the American health care system and its practitioners as expressed in the text (e.g., chapter 23)? What roles does medical technology play in the American system of illness and health, particularly with regard to the elderly? What role can or should private or public agencies play in addressing this issue? What is the relationship of diverse American attitudes toward "socialized medicine" to important American cultural values, as illustrated, for example, in the recent contentious debates about medical reform?

8. How would you describe the American class system as it appears through the characters, settings, social interactions, and dialogue in the text (e.g., chapters 5, 6, 9, 21–23, and 25)? What are some of the criteria of the different social classes? What are some of the various attitudes toward the American class system expressed by the characters (chapters 16, 19, and 21–23)? What is your attitude? What is the role of spatial segregation in maintaining the American class system?

9. What are some American attitudes toward illness, pain, death, and dying as expressed throughout the novel (e.g., chapters 11, 14, and 18)? How do religious beliefs, funeral rituals, the transfer of organs and tissues, and ordinary behaviors, such as smoking or food choices, reflect American culture regarding these issues? How does American culture differ from other cultures in this regard (e.g., chapters 15 and 18)?

10. What are some possible relationships between art and death? Why might various cultures, in different ways, use art to send messages about death and dying? Based on your reactions to the different materials used in the art described at the museum exhibits (chapter 12), would you say dead things are always repulsive? What elements make them so? Can death be made beautiful? How might that happen? What art exhibits, films, theater performances, or literature on death and dying have shaped your views on these subjects?

11. What are some of the common threads among the immigrants that appear in the text? What lessons have their life experiences taught

them (e.g., chapters 1, 11, and 13)? What aspects of American culture, if any, do you think immigrants should be compelled to conform to? Which aspects of their traditional cultures can they retain and still adapt successfully as Americans? How does your response apply to nonimmigrant minorities such as Native Americans or African Americans (chapters 24 and 25)? In your opinion, is multiculturalism a good thing or a major problem for the United States? Explain with reference to the novel (e.g., chapters 1, 9, and 13, and the epilogue).

12. Concepts of law, law enforcement, crime, justice, and professional ethics are central to American culture and social behavior. What are some of the different motives for unethical, illegal, or seriously criminal behavior expressed in our story (e.g., chapters 1, 13, 21, 25, and 26)? What are some of the dominant American methods of dealing with crime and perceived injustice as revealed in the novel (e.g., chapters 11, 17, 18, and 20)? Ernesto (chapter 26) and Mike (chapter 20) both suggest that popular television entertainment encourages "magical thinking" about crime and justice in contrast to the realities of the criminal justice system. Explain why you agree or disagree.

13. Central to American culture is our emphasis on economic development through industrial capitalism, corporatism, and entrepreneurship; public support of education, the military, and public works, such as highways and national parks (e.g., chapters 23 and 24); and subsidies for economic activities, such as agriculture, tourist development, and the arts. Discuss the benefits and problems of various forms of economic development (e.g., chapters 21, 24, and 25). How has this played out in your region of the country?

14. Cultures and societies are always changing, in both small and large ways. Describe some current cultural changes occurring globally (e.g., chapters 3, 7, and 10) and how these are affecting aging and eldercare in different cultures. What are some of the demographic, political, economic, social, and other changes that are affecting American society as presented in the text (e.g., chapters 2, 23, and 24)? With reference to the novel's plot, characters, and setting, discuss how these changes may affect American culture in the future, particularly regarding concepts of health, illness, death, and dying.

 Glossary

American Dream	The widespread belief in the opportunity for all Americans to achieve upward social mobility from one class to another through education, hard work, and risk taking
applied anthropology/ sociology	The application of the knowledge from anthropology and sociology to the solution of human problems
brain dead	Complete cessation of brain function as evidenced by the absence of brain wave activity on an electroencephalogram; sometimes used as a legal definition of death
calalou	A Haitian dish made of onions, okra, spinach, peppers, crabmeat, and salted pork
capitalism	An economic system in which land and capital goods are privately owned, capital is invested for profit, and people work for wages
carpe diem	Latin for "seize the day"
(social) class	The division of people into groups with differing access to resources
class system	A form of social stratification in which the different strata form a continuum and social mobility is possible from one class to another

culture	The knowledge, language, values, norms (established rules of behavior or standards of conduct), and material objects shared by members of a particular society
cultural anthropology	The subfield of anthropology that deals with the many forms, expressions, and practices of culture
cultural relativity	The idea that each society or culture must be understood on its own terms
denial	In psychology, an unconscious defense mechanism used to reduce anxiety by denying thoughts, feelings, or facts that are consciously intolerable
Dios te lo da y Dios te lo quita	Spanish for "God gives and God takes away"
fieldwork/ ethnography	The anthropological method of studying culture through long-term participant observation
(Florida) Gold Coast	The eastern seacoast towns and cities from Miami to Jupiter
halal	Anything legal for Muslims to use, as in permitted foods
medical anthropology	A subfield of cultural anthropology concerned with the ways in which disease is understood and treated in different cultures
medical culture	The culture of the institutionalized system of medicine, which includes the scientific diagnosis, treatment, and prevention of illness
mezuzah	In common usage, refers to a small metal case containing verses from Deuteronomy in the Hebrew Bible that some Jewish people affix to their doorpost
pain patate	A sweetened potato, fig, and banana pudding
reciprocity	The exchange of goods and services between people without the use of money
segregation	The spatial and social separation of categories of people by race, ethnicity, class, or religion

social stratification	The hierarchical arrangement of large social groups based on their control over basic resources
status	A socially defined position in a society
subculture	A group of people who share a distinctive set of cultural beliefs and behaviors that differs in some significant way from that of the larger society
WASP	The Women Airforce Service Pilots, active in World War II
yogi	Hindu holy man

Bibliographic Essay

This essay includes our references and serves as a guide to sources for further investigation of some of the major topics in our book in the order in which they appear.

Henry Flagler, the man who started it all, is the subject of David Chandler's *Henry Flagler: The Astonishing Life and Times of the Visionary Robber Baron Who Founded Florida* (New York: Macmillan, 1986).

Chapter 1 introduces the controversial subject of tissue and organ markets, a million-dollar domestic and international industry that has become subject to fraud, exploitation, and violence. Two anthropological sources are Leslie A. Sharp's "Commodified Kin: Death, Mourning, and Competing Claims on the Bodies of Organ Donors in the United States," *American Anthropologist* 103 (2001): 112–33; and Nancy Scheper-Hughes's "The Global Traffic in Human Organs," *Current Anthropology* 41, no. 2 (2000): 191–223. The Internet offers much information on organ and tissue donation; for just one of the many cases of illegal activity, referred to in chapter 1, see Michael Brick's "4 Men Charged in What Officials Call a $4.6 Million Trade in Human Body Parts," *New York Times*, February 24, 2006, B4.

Dr. Paul Farmer is the author of *Pathologies of Power: Health, Human Rights and the New War on the Poor* (Berkeley: University of California

Press, 2003) and is the subject of Tracy Kidder's *Mountains beyond Mountains: The Quest of Dr. Paul Farmer, a Man Who Would Cure the World* (New York: Random House, 2003). An anthropological examination of "car culture" is found in Catherine Lutz and Anne Lutz Fernandez's *Carjacked: The Culture of the Automobile and Its Effects on our Lives* (New York: Palgrave/MacMillan, 2010).

A compelling read on the culture of the Jewish elderly is Barbara Myerhoff's *Number Our Days: A Triumph of Continuity and Culture among Jewish Old People in an Urban Ghetto* (New York: Simon and Schuster, 1979). Norman H. Gershman, in *BESA: Muslims Who Saved Jews in World War II* (Syracuse, N.Y.: University of Syracuse Press, 2008), explores *besa*, the Albanian principle of offering protection to those who need it, expressed in the life stories of now elderly Jews saved from the Holocaust. Cultural perspectives on aging in America are also the subject of Margaret Morganroth Gullette's *Aged by Culture* (Chicago: University of Chicago Press, 2004); and Luisa Margolies's *My Mother's Hip: Lessons from the World of Eldercare* (Philadelphia: Temple University Press, 2004). These are helpfully reviewed in Sarah Lamb's "Critical Investigations of Age and Aging in the United States," *American Anthropologist* 107, no. 4 (2005): 705–8. Dr. Robert Butler, who coined the word "ageism," wrote the pathbreaking book that revolutionized negative stereotypes of aging in America: *Why Survive? Being Old in America* (New York: Harper and Row, 1975). Joan Wile's *Grandmothers against the War: How We Got Off Our Fannies and Stood Up for Peace* (New York: Kensington Press, 2008) contains moving oral histories of senior peace activists.

Demographic and health statistics on aging are available on the website of the National Institute on Aging. Another important Internet site is www.medicare.gov/. Florida's Department of Elder Affairs describes the Communities for a Lifetime program, a comprehensive effort to encourage independent living by older people, such as increasing police investigation of fraud and enabling pedestrian safety.

Aging and eldercare in other cultures are described in editors Dorothy Ayers Counts and David R. Counts's *Aging and Its Transformations: Mov-*

ing toward Death in Pacific Societies (Lanham, Md.: University Press of America, 1985); John W. Traphagan's "Contesting the Transition to Old Age in Japan," *Ethnology* 37, no. 4 (1998): 333–50; Howard W. French's "Rush for Wealth in China's Cities Shatters the Ancient Assurance of Care in Old Age," *New York Times*, November 3, 2006, A8; Dan Levin's "Tradition Under Stress," *AARP Bulletin* (July/August 2008); Lynette Clemetson's "US Muslims Confront Taboo on Nursing Homes," *New York Times* June 13, 2006, A1; Harriet G. Rosenberg's "Complaint Discourse: Aging and Caregiving among the Ju/'hoansi," in *The Dobe Ju/'hoansi*, edited by Richard B. Lee, 3rd ed., 91–102 (Belmont, Calif.: Wadsworth, 2003); Jay Sokolovsky's *The Cultural Context of Aging: Worldwide Perspectives* (New York: Bergin and Garvey, 2009); and Sokolovsky's "Aging, Center Stage: New Life Course Research in Anthropology," *Anthropology News* 50, no. 8 (November 2009): 5–8. See also "The AAA Aging and Life Course Interest Group Guide to Key Resources," at www.stpt.usf.edu/~jsokolov/ageguide .htm (accessed December 5, 2010). Various aspects of aging in Indian culture are described in Rohinton Mistry's *Family Matters* (New York: Knopf, 2002); Lawrence Cohen's *No Aging in India: Alzheimer's, the Bad Family, and Other Modern Things* (Berkeley: University of California Press, 1998); and Sarah Lamb's *Aging and the Indian Diaspora: Cosmopolitan Families in India and Abroad* (Bloomington: University of Indiana Press, 2009).

Retirement in the United States is the subject of Joel Savishinsky's *Breaking the Watch: The Meanings of Retirement in America* (Ithaca, N.Y.: Cornell University Press, 2000). *Sunset Daze*, a new reality television show set in a retirement community, is reviewed by Alessandra Stanley, in "The Golden Years: Feisty, Fit and Flirty," *New York Times*, April 28, 2010, C4. The show's vision of retirement as the "sky-diving grandma" is explored by Kate Zernike, in "Turn 70: Act Your Grandchild's Age," *New York Times*, July 11, 2001; she presents statistics on debility and illness related to aging as they affect ordinary people.

Many websites and several university archives contain historical and contemporary information on the WASP, the Women Airforce Service Pilots of World War II.

Artistic representations of death are found in David Revere McFadden and Lowery Stokes Sims's 2010 exhibit "Dead or Alive," Museum of Art and Design, New York; the catalog for the 2010 exhibit "Remember That You Will Die: Death across Cultures," Rubin Museum of Art, New York; and new, permanent exhibits on Egyptian views of death at the Brooklyn Museum, New York, and the Bass Museum in Miami Beach. End-of-life issues are the focus of the 2010 television film *You Don't Know Jack: The Life and Deaths of Jack Kevorkian*, about a physician associated with assisted suicide in the United States. See also Thomas Lynch's *Apparitions and Late Fictions: A Novella and Stories* (New York: Norton, 2010); and *Let Me Down Easy*, a one-woman theater piece by Anna Deavere Smith (2009). For an overview of death and dying in the United States from a practitioner's point of view, see editors Barbara A. Backer, Natalie Hannon, and Noreen A. Russell's *Death and Dying: Understanding and Care*, 2nd ed. (Albany, N.Y.: Delmar, 1994). The reference to attitudes toward dying in Japan is from Ian Buruma's "The Mystery of Female Grace," *New York Review of Books*, May 27, 2010.

On cross-cultural funeral ritual, see Serena Nanda's "Death from a Cross-Cultural Perspective," in *Death and Dying: Understanding and Care*, edited by Barbara A. Backer, Natalie Hannon, and Noreen A. Russell, 2nd ed., 313–37 (Albany, N.Y.: Delmar, 1994); Richard Huntington and Peter Metcalf's *Celebrations of Death: The Anthropology of Mortuary Ritual* (Cambridge: Cambridge University Press, 1979); and Paul C. Rosenblatt, R. Patricia Walsh, and Douglas A. Jackson's *Grief and Mourning in Cross-Cultural Perspective* (New Haven, Conn.: HRAF Press, 1976). In "Why We Want Their Bodies Back," *Discover Magazine*, February 2002, Robert Sapolsky examines the extreme lengths Americans go to in order to retrieve the dead, while Frank Rich, in "A Culture of Death, Not Life," *New York Times*, April 10, 2005, 4:13, explores death as a television spectacle in the Terry Schiavo case in Florida.

American medical culture is discussed in Roland Littlewood's *On Knowing and Not Knowing in the Anthropology of Medicine* (Walnut Creek, Calif.: Left Coast Press, 2009); Jerome Groopman's "Diagnosis: What Doctors Are Missing," *New York Review of Books*, November 5, 2009; and Groopman's "Dilemmas for Doctors," *New York Review of Books*, December 17, 2009. For an objective view of what the current health care reforms actually involve, see Jonathan Oberlander and Theodore Marmon's "The Health Bill Explained at Last," *New York Review of Books*, August 19, 2010. The "magical thinking" in American culture regarding illness and the cultures of health-related institutions is explored in Barbara Ehrenreich's *Brightsided: How the Relentless Promotion of Positive Thinking Has Undermined America* (New York: Metropolitan Books, 2009).

An ethnography of gated communities in urban America, which includes a useful bibliography, is Setha M. Low's "The Edge and the Center: Gated Communities and the Discourse of Urban Fear," *American Anthropologist* 103, no. 1 (2001): 45–58.

On the Everglades, see Don Van Natta Jr. and Damien Cave's "Deal to Save Everglades May Help Sugar Firm," *New York Times*, March 8, 2010, A1; and the PBS television special "The National Parks: America's Best Idea," by Ken Burns, which has a segment on the Everglades. See also Alec Wilkinson's *Big Sugar: Seasons in the Cane Fields of Florida* (New York: Knopf, 1989); and Jessica R. Cattelino's *High Stakes: Florida Seminole Gaming and Sovereignty* (Durham, N.C.: Duke University Press, 2008).

For cultural diversity in South Florida, see David Rieff's *The Exile: Cuba in the Heart of Miami* (New York: Simon and Schuster, 1993); and Rieff's *Going to Miami: Exiles, Tourists, and Refugees in the New America* (Boston: Little, Brown, 1987). Crime on the Gold Coast is described in Gerald Posner's *Miami Babylon: Crime, Wealth, and Power—a Dispatch from the Beach* (New York: Simon and Schuster, 2009); the archives of the Historical Museum of Southern Florida, at www.hmsf.org/collections-home.htm (accessed June 20, 2010); Edna Buchanan's *The Corpse Had a Familiar Face: Covering Miami, America's Hottest Beat* (New York: Random House, 1987); and, with special reference to the elderly, Joe Roubicek's *Financial Abuse of the Elderly: A Detective's Case Files of Exploitation Crimes* (n.p.: Ruby House Publications, 2008).

On an English serial killer of the elderly, see Brian Whittle and Jean Ritchie's *Harold Shipman: Prescription for Murder* (London: Time

Warner, 2004); and Mikaela Sitford's *Serial Killer File: The Doctor of Death Investigation* (New York: Bearport, 2007). *CSI: Miami*, the subject of several novels and a television series, is analyzed in Corinna Kruse's "Producing Absolute Truth: CSI as Wishful Thinking," *American Anthropologist* 112, no. 1 (2010): 79–91. Zoe Crossland, in "Of Clues and Signs: The Dead Body and Its Evidential Traces," *American Anthropologist* 111, no. 1 (2009): 69–80, explores forensic science and forensic anthropology in their historical context.

About the Authors

Serena Nanda, PhD, anthropology, is professor emeritus at John Jay College of Criminal Justice, City University of New York. She is widely known for her comparative ethnographic work on gender diversity, marriage and family, and American multiculturalism and law. She is the coauthor of *Cultural Anthropology* (tenth edition, 2009); *Culture Counts: A Concise Introduction to Cultural Anthropology* (second edition, 2010); and *American Cultural Pluralism and Law* (with Jill Norgren, 2006). Her other works include *Gender Diversity: Crosscultural Variation* and, with Joan Gregg, *The Gift of a Bride: A Tale of Anthropology, Matrimony, and Murder* (2009).

Joan Gregg, PhD, comparative literature, is professor emeritus at New York City College of Technology, City University of New York. She is the author of *Devils, Women, and Jews: Reflections of the Other in Medieval Sermon Stories* (1997) and the coauthor of many English as a Second Language textbooks used in both the United States and Asia. She has taught English literature and English as a Foreign Language to teachers and college students in Pakistan, China, Indonesia, Vietnam, and Malaysia. She is the coauthor of a New York City guidebook, *40 Perfect New York Days*, with Serena Nanda and Beth Pacheco (2004).